DO YOU BELIEVE IN
LIFE AFTER LOSS?

of related interest

The Queer Mental Health Workbook
A Creative Self-Help Guide Using CBT, CFT and DBT
Dr Brendan J. Dunlop
ISBN 978 1 83997 107 5
eISBN 978 1 83997 108 2

The Trans Guide to Mental Health and Well-Being
Katy Lees
ISBN 978 1 78775 526 0
eISBN 978 1 78775 527 7

Meet Me There, Another Time
Letters to Places that Queer and Trans People Left Behind
Lexie Bean
ISBN 978 1 80501 221 4
eISBN 978 1 80501 222 1

Coming Out Stories
Personal Experiences of Coming Out from
Across the LGBTQ+ Spectrum
Edited by Emma Goswell and Sam Walker
ISBN 978 1 78775 495 9
eISBN 978 1 78775 496 6

Do You Believe in Life After Loss?

Queer Stories of Loss, Hope and Resilience

Andrew Flewitt

Jessica Kingsley Publishers
London and Philadelphia

First published in Great Britain in 2025 by Jessica Kingsley Publishers
An imprint of John Murray Press

1

A CIP catalogue record for this title is available from the British Library and the Library of Congress

ISBN 978 1 80501 770 7
eISBN 978 1 80501 771 4

Printed and bound in Great Britain by Clays Ltd

Jessica Kingsley Publishers' policy is to use papers that are natural, renewable and recyclable products and made from wood grown in sustainable forests. The logging and manufacturing processes are expected to conform to the environmental regulations of the country of origin.

Jessica Kingsley Publishers
Carmelite House
50 Victoria Embankment
London EC4Y 0DZ

www.jkp.com

John Murray Press
Part of Hodder & Stoughton Ltd
An Hachette Company

The authorised representative in the EEA is Hachette Ireland,
8 Castlecourt Centre, Dublin 15, D15 XTP3, Ireland (email: info@hbgi.ie)

For anyone who has experienced or is dealing with loss, I hope you find this book inspiring. And for anyone who has had to step beyond expectations and choose a different path in their life, this is for you.

Contents

Part 2: Reflections and Resources

Introduction

Let's get going with stating the obvious; loss is an inevitable reality of life, something that we will all face in various ways and at different times throughout our lives. Perhaps this is not what you want to read when you're starting a new book; I appreciate it may not be seen as an exciting hook, but please do go on. I promise it is not all doom and gloom and it is for this very reason I wanted to write the book.

In 2023, I experienced personal change in my life, which, you've guessed it, involved loss. If someone had told me a year ago that I would be writing a book about loss following the death of a parent, the ending of a family dynamic and a separation from my partner, I think I would have done whatever I could have mentally to reject the very prospect of these situations becoming my reality. Control is something I have come to realize is fruitless, and frankly a waste of energy. We have very little control over most things in life, especially when it comes to endings, and the grand plan that life has in store for us. Scary, right?

When meeting with a therapist in the summer of 2023 to talk about the changes and loss I had experienced, I also discussed situations that I believed I had healed from, because they came up as a natural part of a conversation. I found myself right back in a difficult situation that I had experienced in 2007, feeling the emotion as if it was happening right then and there. The therapist stopped one of our sessions and said, 'Andrew, you have had to deal with a lot of loss and endings in your life.' He was surprised and wanted to take a moment to acknowledge this. I didn't have an answer for this statement; I just agreed.

Maybe the loss I have experienced throughout my life has provided an internal resilience to face future challenges that I didn't know I had? I have spent so much of my life in my head trying to control situations, so that nothing went wrong, that maybe I didn't realize that I had this resilience stored to help me when I really needed it. This got me thinking whether this is a common trend for other queer people; do we have internal resilience because of our experiences with finding ourselves and growing up queer? Or do we become more resilient as we navigate life because of the situations we encounter, including loss, that continue to shape us and how we approach and navigate life as time goes on?

After speaking with my therapist, I now understand that I did experience loss from a young age, and even if I didn't understand it at the time, it shaped me, how I perceive the world and how I live my life, and has continued to do so throughout adulthood. When I was six years old, my brother passed away, something that was very painful for my dad. I was too young to remember him or understand what had happened. Dad couldn't talk about it because it was just too painful. As a child, I would often want to ask questions, trying to get my head around the events that led to a brother I had, but couldn't remember, dying, but as soon as I brought up the topic or even said his name, Dad would shut down. As an adult, I understand how much pain he was in, but he just didn't know how to express this in a healthy way, so he locked it in, and did a really good job with that for the rest of his life.

When you're a kid and a life event like this takes place, it changes things and hangs over you like a dark cloud. You think you want to understand and process it, but it was just ignored. I didn't realize it at the time, but looking back, I think this situation made me fear the unknown. I hated not being in control, and now with having a clinical diagnosis of obsessive compulsive disorder (OCD), which started when I was about seven or eight years old (although no one, including me, knew or understood this), I quietly became scared of death.

I worried constantly that my nana would die if I didn't complete certain rituals, like kissing her picture good night before I went to bed, or turning the light on and off. Her door number was 48, so I would do things in fours or eights as part of my rituals. We went to my grandfather's grave (he died when I was two years old) a lot throughout my childhood, with my dad and nana, and I became aware from looking at the gravestone that he died at 70 years old. I would calculate the maths so

I would know when my dad would die, as I thought this was the age typically when people passed away. My nana was older than 70, so I feared her dying all the time, but we were very lucky that we had her until she was 95 years old. I remember worrying about this stuff all the time. It eased as I got into my teens, but at that point, my OCD had manifested in other ways, and looking back I think my mind was always on high alert and looking for danger.

In 2007, I lost a very dear friend to me, through circumstances which were and still are just unfathomable. I won't go into this, because it isn't my story to tell, and I also want to be respectful to my friend's family, but this life event shaped so much of my twenties. Looking back, I was poorly with my OCD; I just didn't really know what to do about it and hoped it would get better, but it didn't! After the loss of my friend, my mental health plummeted. I didn't know how to manage my grief and I became very depressed. I didn't have the emotional intelligence or experience to process this loss and it consumed my life. People around me were sympathetic, but after a while they were bored listening to me talking about it and bored with me being sad. My relationships at work became difficult, I felt alone most days when I was in the office, and I felt like a burden. The truth is, I was very unhappy. I was depressed and my OCD was at its worst. I worried and obsessed about everything, and when you feel isolated, insecure and paranoid, it makes the compulsions, which are a major factor of the condition, so much worse. Day-to-day life at times was hell, and I am not exaggerating when I say that looking back I honestly don't know how I managed to get through it.

As a result of this experience, I became terrified of losing my partner. He would go out by himself, and I worried that he would not come back. He travelled for work, and I would be beside myself, praying to I don't know who in the shower to keep him safe. I stopped going out and lost interest in the things I loved, because I was depressed but also because I was insecure and didn't want to leave the bubble that we had created that I found safe. Life had changed so dramatically for my friend and her family, and no one expected it, so if something bad could happen to them, what could happen to mine? There is no doubt in my mind how hard this was for my partner, and over time it became suffocating for both of us and contributed to an element of co-dependency in our relationship. Loss shapes us even if we don't understand it; it is only when you can look back and truly face what happened that you can understand the impact of the situation and learn from these experiences.

I look back on these situations and their effects on my life with compassion – for myself, the small frightened child, and for all these emotions they didn't understand, and for the adult who tried their best, undoubtedly made mistakes, but really did the best they could. It is so easy to punish ourselves when life is difficult, or when events in life cause us to feel a certain way. I remember in my twenties feeling so broken, wishing that I didn't feel like I did, and trying to be okay, but I now know that we cannot think ourselves out of these situations. It isn't possible to control everything in life, or our reactions to life events; usually our reactions are a result of our experiences, and the events and environments that have shaped us, whether we understand this or not.

As I approach my forties, I now understand the importance of running towards the pain rather than away from it. By doing this, we not only understand more about the situations we find ourselves in, but we can be kinder to ourselves, feel the emotions we are experiencing and move forward with life. I once told a friend that you need to go through the mud to become a flower, which is the kind of generic statement you might find on a tea towel! I have no idea where I heard this, I think it was my own spin on another analogy, which I heard or saw somewhere, but as I sit here writing this, it makes so much sense to me, more now than ever. The losses I experienced in 2023 came in very quick succession and were difficult. It wasn't until I took a break in the summer of 2023, and had no agenda for 12 weeks, that I started to process what had happened and the feelings I was carrying. With time, patience and lots of therapy throughout the year, things started to get easier. I remember waking up one morning, thinking about everything that had happened, and deciding that I could sink or I could swim and turn the difficulties into something that could help me and maybe others too. In that moment, the concept of a book was born, and the title came to me: *Do You Believe in Life After Loss?*

It seems strange to me that even in difficult times, we can have our biggest inspiration, and creative ideas can present themselves, but as odd as this may be, I am incredibly grateful. Creativity has not only helped me heal, but I also now understand it is essential for my well-being. Creativity gives me focus and purpose; it lifts me up when I feel down, and even when I am out of resources and want to do anything but be creative, I know I will feel so much better if I just do something.

Initially, I intended to write something that helped me process the challenges that 2023 presented, and I did, but that book is in the draft pile. It wasn't a wasted effort, as writing enabled me to tap into my thoughts and feelings and process them, but I then got thinking about the topic of loss generally, beyond my own personal experiences, and how sharing our stories and talking openly really does help more than we know. We will all have our experiences when it comes to loss in our lives, and since embarking on this journey of writing I have learned that loss can feature in the everyday things that we deal with and isn't just limited to events such as a parent dying or losing a partner, heartbreaking as those situations can be.

I'm conscious of the fact that as queer people, we get to step out of the box of rules that society generally has laid out, and make our own; in fact, we don't need rules, we just have to be ourselves, and choose how we want to live our lives in the most authentic way we can. This is not always easy, but it is common, and the stories in this book that pertain to experiences of loss and moving forward with life, even when the chips are down, will inspire you and wherever you may be in this regard. This book explores different aspects of loss, the challenges of these situations, but also the opportunities that have arisen when healing has begun. You will read inspiring stories from people within the queer community, and there are contributions from psychotherapist Silva Neves throughout.

Things will happen in life that may result in a loss being felt, but we don't realize or cannot articulate our feelings as this – we simply brush ourselves off and carry on with life. It isn't until later down the line that we may be able to identify the feelings and the impact of this trauma, because we can no longer hide away our emotions. I've been there and I know others have too. When you dive further into this book, you will understand the loss many contributors have felt with regard to their identity, intimacy, cultural and religious community, among other things.

Tapping into my optimistic state (I tend to be one of those people!), let's consider the queer community and the resilience we have. I think we have this resilience because we have had to find it within, pure and simple. Understanding who we are, living our truth, especially in the world today, can be tough and exhausting. It isn't just about individual experiences that we face as queer people; collectively we are affected by the experiences of others, and it can weigh on us all even if what is happening or being written about isn't directly about us as individuals. I don't need to tell you of the global fight that continues for equality for our community, or that transgender rights, conversion therapy and many other things are still a topic of debate, which is so upsetting to write. When we're faced with salacious headlines, false information and stories being reported, and the fact that we, our lives and who we are should be a topic of debate, an internal resilience is built, even if we don't realize it, because we need to take care of ourselves and keep going, as we have always had to.

Loss is tough, it can be heartbreaking and complex to navigate, but I believe there is hope. We all have our own stories and will be at different stages of processing the loss we may be feeling, but I hope this book recognizes that we are not alone, that so many of us are dealing with challenges that may not only be testing, but at times exhausting. Sometimes, it feels as if things will never be the same again, and that the despair and struggle are too much, but being brave and facing the darkest moments can also provide opportunities. With time, new chapters can be created. It is not always easy, but it is possible.

The interviews in this book discuss how people have dealt with loss in their lives; we look at what they have learned from their experiences, how these experiences have shaped them and whether they believe that there is life after loss.

What I have come to realize is that there is no right or wrong way to grieve or process loss, or in fact move forward with life when you are ready to do so; we all must navigate this in a way that feels appropriate and comfortable to us individually. My early experience of loss and the experiences I have had as a queer person throughout my life helped me in navigating the challenging situations that 2023 brought to me. I wonder if other queer people will have felt the same based on their own personal experiences. Let's find out!

A note on terminology

You will notice at times that I use the term queer community, rather than the LGBTQIA+ (lesbian, gay, bisexual, transgender, queer, intersex, asexual and others) community, throughout the book and I would like to provide a little context. Queer is a word that for many years was used as a weapon against me and many other people within our community. It was seen as a negative slur, or a term of ridicule, and I know having spoken to people in the community over recent years that it is a word that some still find offensive and very difficult to use.

I personally have reclaimed this word and feel that identifying as queer enables my sexuality, sex, gender identity and expression the freedom I have craved for many years; in essence, it gives me an opportunity to reduce labels, step out of binaries and boxes and live freely. It is still work in progress, but it really has helped me with accepting all the different facets of who I am. I do appreciate that not everyone will feel this way, but I do hope that referencing the queer community will not deter people from engaging in the incredible stories that are shared within this book.

PART 1
Queer Stories of Loss, Hope and Resilience

CHAPTER 1

Loss of Identity

Nathaniel J. Hall

Age: 37
Pronouns: He/They
Sexual orientation/identity: Gay
Occupation: Actor, writer and HIV activist
Home town: Salford, UK

Nathaniel J. Hall is an award-winning writer, performer and HIV activist known for his stigma-smashing shows First Time *and* Toxic. *His community-led creative activism has directly reached over tens of thousands through creative workshops and talks, and tens of millions through broadcast media and print. He appeared as Donald Bassett in the hit C4 drama* It's a Sin *and recently fronted a documentary for C4 on the HIV subculture of bug chasing. Nathaniel is Artistic Director of Dibby Theatre, an LGBTQ+ touring theatre company based in Salford.*

In this interview, I speak with Nathaniel about their experience of a loss of identity, following their HIV diagnosis. Please be aware that this interview makes references to abuse (mental and physical), poor mental health, post-traumatic stress disorder (PTSD), sex, shame and stigma.

How do you tend to manage an ending or a loss when it's presented to you?

I really enjoy endings. My favourite season is autumn, because there's something about the dying and decaying of the natural world and that cycle that's powerful. Autumn is camp, do you know what I mean? She's cute, she's like all kinds of colours of the rainbow and intense, and it's obviously lovely to go for walks and all that stuff. There's just something about this idea that everything comes to an end. I like change, and I don't like things to stay the same. My two favourite seasons are spring and autumn, because they're seasons of change.

In autumn, the trees, the leaves, and the flowers that grew that season end, they die, and they go back into the earth and back into the soil. Autumn reminds me of my grandparents who I've lost, or friends who have died, and it's a very reflective time. So, I really enjoy endings. I think that comes from doing a lot of work, thinking, reflecting, and facing my own mortality, and accepting that this is not forever.

I don't get upset by endings, which I think is something people find tricky. When you've got over the initial upset of a relationship ending, whether it's a friendship or a romantic one, and you look back and realize it was for the right reasons, there's something quite calming about that. I've never been a person who holds on to friendships just because that's what you do; my thoughts are that I gave you what you needed at that time, and you gave me what I needed – we don't need to force it beyond that. That's a natural ending for me, and I guess as I'm a playwright, every story I tell must have an ending, and they're hard. You must wrestle with the ending and you must understand that the end is coming; it's important within a story to realize that nothing is permanent.

Can you talk to me about your experience of a loss of identity?
The first one was after I was diagnosed with HIV when I was 16. That was in 2003, when I was in the closet at school, I was still trying to come to terms with my sexuality and trying to understand and pick at the internalized homophobia that was coming from the external homophobia I was witnessing.

I had a fling with someone while I was still at school, but nothing was open, it was all covered up and I had girlfriends to cover it up too. I didn't feel that there were any role models or anyone I identified with, then I met someone and suddenly it all made sense. Everything that I was feeling and that I'd suppressed, things like not reaching for that t-shirt or those jeans because people at school or even my brothers, unintentionally, would shame me because it wasn't what you wore as a man. Suddenly, I could do these things. I threw myself into that and it felt exciting, exhilarating, thrilling and validating, but it was secret because I was still trying to work out how to come out to my parents. It was my first sexual experience and from that I contracted HIV.

I remember being at school in sex education a couple of years prior to this, where the only gay sex education we had – bearing in mind Section 28 was still in place – was delivered by a maths teacher, totally out of their depth for heterosexual sex education, never mind gay sex education. They wheeled out the TV on the trolley with the strap across the top, and put on a video about HIV and AIDS, and in this documentary there was a gay man who was dying from AIDS.

The video was out of date because effective HIV medication came in around 1996 and there was no reference to that. So, we were getting this out-of-date information. I was sat there coming to terms with my sexuality and understanding that I didn't want to *be* like Keanu Reeves in *The Matrix*, I wanted to be *with* Keanu Reeves. We all sat there watching this video, that essentially said don't be gay because you'll get AIDS and die. That was the message, loud and clear.

It was about trying to say, be careful, but without any kind of other talk about being gay, that was the only message we were getting. I remember sitting at the front of the class, feeling that there were 27 pairs of eyes burning into the back of my neck. I could feel it in my body, staying almost stuck and still, trying not to flinch, trying not to show that I identified in any way with what I was seeing on screen.

So that was a powerful moment, and then two years later, just as I was blossoming into my sexuality, essentially the prophecy came true. It was as if I dipped my toe in the gay world and got what I deserved. These experiences had a powerful impact on how I continued with my identity as a queer person and how as I developed, that impacted every aspect of my life, my relationship with my family, my relationship with my friends and partners.

It also affected my relationship with myself; I got into alcohol, drugs, sex, the lot, all through the framework of the intense stigma and shame I felt about being gay and living with HIV.

Did the loss of identity mean that you were hiding yourself from other people, or hiding truly what was going on in your life?

Well, I think what happened at that point was a personality split. I very much stepped through the motions of what it meant to come out and be loud and proud. I was starting my early activism, writing about what the Bible says about homosexuality in the college newsletter, magazine and all that sort of stuff, and going out on Canal Street into that gay world and dressing the way I wanted. So, I guess in a sense that carried on. But the other version of me was drowning in secrecy and shame. Over time, the lack of addressing that trauma, and the impact of that trauma, led to my diagnosis of complex post-traumatic stress disorder and generalized anxiety, about 15 years later in life. So, there was a kind of splitting.

I guess at that point you're making a transition, when your childhood self is going and you're stepping into the adult world. We all probably have that moment in our life. For me, it came early on, and it was intense; to be thrown into that world of HIV, sitting in these rooms that were unfamiliar, uninviting and unwelcoming, and feeling it but not saying that I just wanted my mum. I still felt like a child at that age, but I was brought up in quite an independent way, so by the age of 12 I had to cook for my family once a week and was parented in a way that meant I was cleaning my own clothes and preparing to become an adult. I was trying to justify the fact that I wasn't reaching for help, rather than admitting that I was crumbling, and just needed a parent there.

I once drew out a timeline of my life when I was making one of my shows. There was a huge timeline, and I put in these life events and the stuff that was happening in the world, and the music I was listening to. I put them into eras; we talk that way in the gay world anyway, don't we? You know, my villain era or whatever. It was interesting because up until the age of 16, it was called the Golden Years. When I think about my childhood, other than being bullied at school and those later few years in secondary school and struggling with my sexuality, I had a great childhood. It was the feeling of endless summer days, and it was safe and secure. We weren't spoiled, but we never wanted for anything. There were no major illnesses or traumas within my family; but from there, it's like a concrete barrier on the timeline. That's over, you need to grow up.

What was the feeling for you at that time, knowing that was your reality?
Since that point, I was very anxious, and that quickly became my natural state; it's only after having had a lot of therapy, Eye Movement Desensitization and Reprocessing (EMDR), and doing a lot of self-reflection, that I now realize my internal state is not necessarily what everyone else is feeling around me. I thought once you become an adult, that's what it is. My chest was always tight – it's not that way now, but that was the feeling I had.

It started to impact me as I moved into my career as a performer. I was in every school production, I was doing dance classes and by the age of 16, I was moving into semi-professional theatre productions. Everyone was saying I was going to go to drama school and become an actor; suddenly, I couldn't audition. I thought it was that I was not cut out for that higher level because I couldn't contain the nerves, but then realizing it was anxiety and not nerves was very different.

Anxiety is physically not being able to control your sweat,

sensations in the body, a feeling of absolute dread, a feeling of tightness in the chest. So, it's hard to say what that felt like at the time. I think it felt as if there was this duality. There was this version of me that was spiralling out of control, needing help, needing support, and then the other, the masked version, who was confident, self-assured, the person that everyone came to for help and advice. I was always studious, and I threw myself into my studies, becoming a perfectionist, which is, again, something that has come back to bite me in later life, and I guess I'm not alone in that in terms of queer people. I think when you start to understand your queerness, often perfectionism becomes a sort of coping mechanism; I need to over-prove my worth because of this other thing.

Did you have anyone around you at that time that you could talk to, and were you confiding in anyone about your feelings?
My boyfriend at the time knew about my HIV status, but obviously this was before I started on PrEP (pre-exposure prophylaxis) medication. I was not on medication for five of those years, because that was the clinical guidance at the time. You weren't put straight on to medication because it had been previously so toxic and hard on the stomach that they needed to delay as long as possible, to avoid you becoming drug resistant. So, I had five years without medication within a relationship, and the fear and dread of not wanting to pass HIV on. I think of the impact my HIV status had on both of us, at that age, and we didn't have the tools to be able to process that.

You talk about not being on medication and the fear of passing HIV on to your partner. Is there an element here of not only

losing your identity because you were struggling with who you were, and your status, but then you wanted to engage in a relationship, have sex, have a life that you deserved, and you had to worry about not passing on the virus? Did it feel as if a freedom was being robbed from you?

Yes, absolutely. I think if you look at a positive coming out story, you gain an identity and the community, don't you? It's exciting and outside the mainstream; that queer journey can be exciting. For me, what I gained was an identity, but then within that community, quite a marginalized and maligned identity. I was a gay man with HIV.

When I was diagnosed, the conversation around HIV was not like it is today. The way that the queer community responded to HIV historically was fantastic, but back then there was still a lot of stigma. The talk was always about disclosure – this word, this heavy word, disclosure – disclosing your status. There is law around reckless and intentional transmission of HIV, if your sexual partner didn't know you had HIV, which can lead to prosecution under the grievous bodily harm provisions, of the Offences Against the Person Act 1861. So there is all this legal stuff and fear. I was talking to my current partner about what gay tribe I was in, as I've never felt as if I fitted into a tribe. How fucked up is that? You come to your community and suddenly, you've got to fit in one of these slots; well, I'm not an otter because I'm not hairy, and I'm not a gym bro, so who am I? The one I fit into is POZ; I'm like, oh great, you've just reduced me down to a fucking virus.

At the time, what I did was run away from embracing that as part of my identity because I felt so ashamed; it's very hard to describe what being stigmatized feels like. Queer people can probably understand to a degree, but something like HIV is probably the most stigmatized disease in the world. Also, the self-stigma and the fear are extremely powerful, combined with the guilt that people feel and the shame. At a later point in my life, I was ending a relationship, and it was at this time I began to look back at what had happened when I was younger and realize how much shame had controlled my life for 15 years. This was the start of my journey to becoming an HIV activist. I realized that by not talking about it, I was living out that idea that it's a shameful thing. I did feel shame, and the only way to rid myself of that was just talking about it. Whether it was on stage, making a show about it, or just telling myself every single day that having HIV is not something to be ashamed of, you are deserving of love, and you are deserving of the sex and the relationships that you want. Only through doing this and changing the hard wiring, and the process of unlearning of 15 years, did I move away from that shameful identity.

What did life look like for you once you understood what was going on, living your life with those feelings, and understanding the shame you felt? How did you get through that time?
Life on the surface was okay and good. I have had some incredible experiences in my life, and I've been very fortunate. I went to university; I got a first in my degree and then I travelled the world. I've been to places some people only dream of. I was fortunate enough to be from a family where my mum and dad weren't asking me for rent or telling me I needed to get my own place. There was always a place for me to come back to, and they encouraged me to go and see the world and do what I wanted, so I did that. I travelled all around Australia, Thailand, India, Hong Kong and Indonesia.

I met somebody else, who was not great for me. In fact, I

knew right from the start, the red flags were all there but there was something darkly fascinating about falling down that rabbit hole. I guess in a sense, the reason why I allowed myself to be treated so badly in that relationship was because I didn't like myself; the longer that relationship went on, the more we became each other's enablers in our self-punishment.

On the surface, I was happy, and everything was the Instagram version of life, all very wonderful, but I've talked about this moment of seeing myself in a mirror, still awake two days after a house party, just looking awful. I look at photographs from that time and I looked dead behind the eyes, as if I'm just a shell. I don't know if anyone else sees it. Maybe it's only me, but I see it.

I was so deeply unhappy, but I was so far down this rabbit hole with this person, and it was that moment where I understood something needed to change because it was going to get very dark. I was never addicted to drugs or alcohol, but I was self-medicating a lot, and on the verge of moving into serious addiction.

I was teetering on the edge of thinking that's not the person I thought I'd become. There's a lot of judgement in that statement and, having been through it, I realize just how easy it is to find yourself in those situations, and why we need compassion for people who do.

Do you think the place you found yourself, and the toxic relationship, took you away from the other feelings you had and just kept spiralling you further into an unhealthy place?
Yeah, it does spiral, and I think part of being in that relationship as well was avoidance, because humans are very good at

avoiding, and we're very good at projecting what we feel about ourselves onto other people.

I can barely believe the relationship happened. There were lots of different elements to it, and lots of situations we found ourselves in, but in my view, my toxicity was not understanding how my expectations were too high for him to achieve, and how staying in that relationship was doing damage to him as well as me.

It was the culmination – I guess the logical and foregone conclusion – of having something psychologically traumatic happen to you at 16 and not dealing with it. I think that people who are locked in unhealthy relationships have often had something that has happened to them that's unresolved. Thankfully, it ended.

How long did it take for that to happen?

Around that time, I decided I needed to process what had happened to me when I was 16, and, ultimately, I needed to tell my family. I tried so many times to tell them and I couldn't; you know, when you get that lump in your throat, it would just never come out. I needed to do something to force me, and so I decided that if I made a show, I was going to have to tell them. I got a commission from a theatre in Greater Manchester, and because the train was leaving the station, there was no going back. I managed to build the courage and force my own hand to tell them.

I made the show, and it was a success, but that's when my relationship exploded; it was bad. I think it was because I was having autonomy away from the relationship, and I was facing up to the things that had happened to me, processing and dealing with them.

Things had come to a head; we were living together, but were not together any more. I went to the Edinburgh Fringe the following year with my show, and I was auditioning for *It's a Sin* around that point; it very much was like, I'm ready to go, because I've tasted something new. I was changing and doing all this self-reflection, and he was sort of falling in the other direction. I came home from Edinburgh, and he'd not sorted anything out. I sold all our furniture in a week, five years' worth of stuff, and moved back in with my mum and dad.

Was it difficult to make the show *Toxic*, knowing the challenges it was born from?
It was very destabilizing because it was something about my core sense of identity that was being disrupted. By dramatizing it and putting it on stage, I was sort of getting a bright torch and shining it on the situation and it was withering away.

Shame and secrecy are interlinked, so if you're shameful about something, you're secretive about it too. For me, the way to rid myself of shame was to not be secretive. We talk about being authentic, don't we? To be congruent to who you are and say, yeah, I'm not perfect, I'm flawed. Yeah, I have done some shit things in my life and shit things have happened to me too, and that's the power for me as an autobiographical storyteller, that's the power of going through those processes. I knew writing and performing *Toxic* would be tough, but it's weird because when you're in it, you don't recognize the shift and the change that it's having until after the fact.

Storytelling is not just in theatre, books and film, but for everyone; going to see a therapist is storytelling. You're creating the story and trying to work it out, giving it a beginning, a middle and an end, knowing that although you've been through things, those things don't define you. That's what the ending is about, isn't it? The ending is about affirming you can close those situations down.

Looking back, it sounds as if you tapped into this new world when you were making and performing *First Time* and told your family about your status. What feelings did you experience at that time? Did you feel braver, and that you were starting to get to know yourself again?
It's hard to say. If I try and put myself back to that time, I'd like to say it's what you're saying there. Maybe you're right, maybe there was a strength coming from understanding that I deserved better, and I wanted better, but I think part of it felt a little bit like running away back to Mum and Dad and having to admit it hadn't gone very well, and I needed to be looked after again.

I'm reticent to put the stamp on it now retrospectively and claim I was really empowered. When I moved out, I still was engaged in a lot of self-harming stuff, a lot of drugs. I went to a sex party, which I'd never done before, and ended up getting a sexually transmitted infection (STI), which was misdiagnosed at the start of the coronavirus pandemic and caused me horrific scarring, because it wasn't treated for six months. It was as if every time I tried and was queer, it fucking came back to bite me.

Looking back at that time, those acts in and of themselves were not and are not shameful, but often people in those situations or engaged in those things are in them because they feel lots of shame, so you've got this toxic soup of people who are not treating themselves well, they're not treating each other well either, and consent and boundaries are really blurred. It's labelled as what queer people do; we absolutely can lead glorious, polyamorous sex lives that put two fingers up at the heteronormative, but at this time for me, shame and secrecy were in the driving seat, not sexual empowerment. I think that can be the case for a lot of us as we're not given the tools to navigate all this.

You've found the strength to move forward, to make art and live more freely. At what point did you start to think, okay, I've got this, life is starting to feel a bit better for me?
It was probably during the COVID pandemic. Most people had a terrible time, but I had a period of rebirth and growth. I worked all the way through the pandemic for not much money, and often for free, but I was trying to use that time wisely. I was very fortunate; I moved back to my parents' house, which was nice because I got to spend three years with them, and our relationship had become distant over the last few years. I was living there rent free, but the deal was I got my life back on track, worked and saved my money.

So, during the pandemic, I threw myself into trauma-based therapy with *We Are Survivors*. I started to acknowledge and label the past relationship as abusive, losing a lot of connections and friends in the process. Again, that was a really painful transition and ending, but understanding and using it, talking about it in that language and not being ashamed of it was important. Through that period, I met my current partner and established that this time I was doing things differently, learning how to communicate and how to state my boundaries and my needs, without accepting anything less than what I deserved.

I filmed *It's a Sin* just before the COVID pandemic, my show *First Time* had just stormed at Edinburgh Fringe and I had all these five-star reviews, and I was just riding the high of that. I'd gone from being in this toxic, awful relationship to playing an on-screen relationship with Olly Alexander, working with Russell T. Davies and going to the Attitude Awards; all these exciting, glamorous things. When I look back, that's the moment where I understood that I deserved to have this stuff, but it was on pause because of everything else. My new partner and I, between us, managed to save enough to buy a house and start a new chapter, but not bury the past. We don't deny that those things are there. I think that's what a lot of people do, they only look forward, but what you've been through defines you. It's important to acknowledge the way these experiences shape you, both the good and bad.

Have you attributed the great things that have happened to you in recent years to being open about who you are, your life and the things you've had to go through?
I went from one extreme to the other. When I made *First Time*, literally no one knew about my HIV status, and then within the space of a week, after launching the show, I'd sat on the BBC Breakfast couch and told the nation. News articles had been shared all over the world and I was getting thousands of messages from people, so it was like zero to a hundred.

It was quite destabilizing, and I didn't undergo an overnight change. I remember after *First Time* having a period of falling back into drugs and alcohol, not on the same level, but I realized that I didn't quite have the processing skills to handle things. The more that you do it, the more you are authentic, the more you accept that this is who you are, you realize it is all okay and that nobody is perfect.

Do you look back on any of the situations that you have experienced with a sense of gratitude and understanding because of where you are in your life right now?

I think we have a sense of our core identity that forms in our teenage and early adult years. There's so much positive to come from my diagnosis, even before I was open about it. I had a sense of my own mortality presented to me at 16; I was told I had 37 years to live, which was oddly specific, but it was a chronic illness at the time I was diagnosed. It was later downgraded to a long-term manageable health condition, but I think if you live with something like HIV, if you're willing to face it head on, it teaches you so much.

I've met other people who live with HIV, who have dealt with and fought this pandemic in the 1980s, have lost lovers and friends, members of ACT UP. I've met the people who were going down to Strangeways Prison in Manchester and putting condoms inside tennis balls and whacking them over the walls, because the prison service in the late 1990s would not give condoms to inmates, and HIV was spreading through the prison population. You know, it's kind of radical. These are just amazing people, and we don't see them, we don't hear about them. They don't get any of the recognition that I get.

People ask me, would you go back, would you change it? I say probably not. Also, if I say that I would change it, that also then says that I've not fully grasped or come to terms with the fact that it's not a shameful thing. I'm going to live a happy, healthy life on medication; it's a little bit more complicated, and yes, getting older is going to be that way too, but it is the same for many people with different conditions.

I was chatting with a Drag Artiste a few weeks ago, and they put it in such a beautiful way: the things that have happened to me don't define who I am, but they have shaped who I've become. That's the important thing; we're all going to face traumatic things in our lives, we're all going to face challenges, whatever they may be, whether they're financial or health-related, and we've all got the ultimate trauma, which is that life is finite. We're all going to have to face that, but there are two ways to move through life; one is to become the hero of your story, and the other is to become the victim. I've sometimes been the victim of my own story and I've wallowed in that, but until you become the hero, until you are willing to take control of your destiny in that sense, you will always look back with shame and remorse.

With your experiences and the way that you've handled these, do you think this approach was unique to you as a queer person? Do you think that someone who doesn't identify as queer would have the same experience?

I think a diagnosis, depending on your identity, of HIV is very different. There is a lot of universality in our experiences, but someone who is Black British or Black African, for example, has a very different lived experience with HIV than I do as a white gay man, and if you're straight it's a very different experience. So, there is a uniqueness in the sense that being queer is magical, and because your very existence is political, even if you're not into politics. The same as if you're Black, or if you're a woman, and you walk into a room, just by entering, you change the energy in that space, and homophobia or transphobia or whatever is at play instantly, whether anyone is openly homophobic.

Homophobia is so pervasive. I had this realization quite a while ago, that homophobia impacts every man alive because it inhibits heterosexual men from being able to be authentic in a lot of cases. For a heterosexual man who wants to dress in a certain way or likes stereotypically gay or queer things, there is so much internalized control that comes from the external homophobia that it shapes. To be queer frees you from that once you've worked through it.

It totally frees you into moving through the world in a different and very exciting way. I've changed from my early and late teens, early twenties, when I was terrified of being queer in public spaces that weren't gay, to absolutely revelling in it. Now I'm walking down that street in my platform shoes, and people are lucky to see this! I'm changing it from being shameful and making it my armour.

How important do you think it is for people to be open about their experiences of loss?
I tell everyone everything, because it's gone very well for me, but I understand that everyone is different and it takes a level of resolve, and stupidity, to decide to turn your life story into a play. There is a freedom in talking about loss. And the minute you start talking about something, you instantly realize that you're not alone, you're not isolated in that experience, or those feelings, and you wonder why you worried so much. I have found that when I ask myself why I won't tell someone something, it always comes back to being ashamed of it and fearing rejection.

Do you feel as a queer person, understanding and exploring your identity, sexuality and your experience of living authentically have enabled you to deal with challenges in life involving change and loss, as and when they arise?

I do think that queer people, or people who label themselves as queer or live in a queer way, have unlocked something about existence and life that other people haven't. That's not to say that they're the only people who have done that, but there's something about understanding queerness deeply that is beyond just sexuality, beyond who you have sex with, or whether you are the gender that you were assigned at birth. There's something magical about doing that, having that level of self-reflection, and then learning to see the world through that lens. The experiences that I've been through – and I've not always labelled myself as queer, although I think I always have been – mean that I've moved through those experiences in a way that's different from other people.

With everything that you've learned so far, what do you think is the most valuable lesson throughout your journey?

Authenticity, learning to be truly authentic. Also, knowing it will pass; you'll get through it when life throws you a curve ball. People always complain about getting older, but it's a blessing, as not everyone makes it, and that's particularly resonant for the gay male generation that came before ours. Even with our generation, we know that rates of suicide are higher in our community, and some don't make it. I don't just mean people who have died, but people who are deeply unhappy, or stuck in cycles of self-abuse or shame, and might be for the rest of their life. Some people do not get a happy fulfilled life and they get to the end of their life and look back and feel it was shit. We know that happiness is a fleeting emotion, not a state of being. When you're not happy, you don't think about being happy for six months at a time, you're just happy when someone makes you laugh or when you have joy. When we're sad or feeling depressed, it may not be forever, it is an emotion that will pass at some point.

Do you believe in life after loss? And how long did it take you to feel that way?

Yes, I do believe in life after loss. They say in terms of a relationship, it takes half the amount of time you're in that relationship to get over the loss of it, so if you're in a relationship for eight years, it's going to take you four years to move forward. That rings quite true for me.

I often talk to friends or family and they tell me they're feeling sad or anxious or depressed. And I look them in the eye and say, yes, but you've just moved house, your dog just died, you just lost a best friend, you just battled a bad illness, give yourself a break! The mind and body need to adjust to the change, and it can take time, but things do and will move forward.

Ask Silva

As an actor and playwright, Nathaniel has created art that has linked directly to their experiences, as discussed within this interview. What is the value of creativity within life, and how can this support in healing when someone has experienced loss?

Creativity is very important in life. Even though psychotherapy is an evidence-based practice, it is also creative, and it is certainly my favourite part of the therapeutic process. Creativity, for some people, may be actually drawing, creative writing, playing music, dancing, cooking and so on. For others, creativity happens when they are attuned to other trusted human beings in the here and now and allowing the flow of the connection.

Much healing happens in those creative moments. Experiencing loss often shakes our grounding and unsettles us. Being unsettled isn't pleasant or desirable at all, but it is also an opportunity to adopt a different philosophy of life as we find our grounding again. Often, it changes us positively and permanently.

For me, for example, surviving the pandemic has changed me forever in a way that I am now so much more aware of my gratitude for being alive, and also aware that life can be short and unpredictable. So, I prioritize what is important for me, and, more crucially, what is full of joy and pleasure. Feeding myself with those moments makes me a better therapist and a more connected person with my chosen family.

CHAPTER 2

Loss of Intimacy

Zachary Tucker

Age: 26
Pronouns: He/Him
Sexual orientation/identity: Gay
Occupation: Recruitment consultant and mental health awareness advocate
Home town: Cardiff, UK

Zack Tucker was born and raised in Cardiff, Wales and has always had a passion for making an impact. The impact has been on the OCD community, using his platform on Instagram, @ocdestigmatize, to eradicate stigma around the highly misunderstood disorder. Zack wanted to make a page that he wished he had access to when he was a child, and now here he is, a few awards later, feeling like he has made some positive change, and raised much needed awareness of a condition that is widely misunderstood.

In this interview, I speak with Zachary about his experience of loss of intimacy, due to a mental health condition, obsessive compulsive disorder (OCD). Please be aware that this interview makes references to drugs, OCD, sexual assault, self-harm, sex and suicide.

How do you tend to manage endings or a loss when it is presented?

I've never really dealt with much loss, but I suppose I'm quite resilient. I'm very strong regarding moving forward or getting on with things.

Can you share with me your personal experience of a loss?

I would describe it as a loss of intimacy due to my mental health condition. I've dealt with loss because of OCD, which has manifested in two main ways. The first way is relationship OCD, so that means any time I enter a relationship, my mind instantly goes to this place of all of these 'what if' questions 24-7. I have thoughts like, 'What if you don't actually like this person?' and 'How can you know for sure?' Before I really knew what it was (a form of OCD), I was just going through relationships and constantly breaking up because any time I entered a relationship my head would just go into a complete spiral. My mind just bombarded me with thoughts, saying things like, 'Oh no, you think this person is ugly, you hate this person, you don't want to be with this person.'

I'd do all these compulsions to tackle that, and I would do romantic gestures to prove to my mind that I did like them. It was just back and forth, and it always ended in me breaking up with the partner, until I found out that I had OCD and then started to work through it. So, I'd say that is the first manifestation of my OCD, and the second is dealing with sexually intrusive thoughts.

These thoughts affected more of the intimacy side of things, sex of any kind. It started when I was about 19 years old, and I would have intrusive thoughts about very taboo subjects, very sexually violent subjects, and this would also follow me into the bedroom. If I was intimate with someone, all I'd be able to think about was these horrible thoughts. I'd also be turned on being with my partner, but my mind made a connection and the OCD questioned whether I was sexually attracted to these thoughts, not the person I was with. So, it really affected my ability to have sex in any form for a very long time.

I hope you don't mind me asking this, but being intimate with yourself, did this become a problem too?
Yes, absolutely. If I was on the computer searching to watch porn, my mind would worry that I would start searching for child porn, or something like that, and then I'd freak out and be like, wait, what if I was going to do that? How do I know I wasn't going to? This sent me into a constant breakdown of self-identity, not really knowing who I was, and not being able to intimately connect with myself or anyone.

How old were you when the OCD started?
It was 2017, so it would have been just before my 20th birthday. It started when I was dating. I'd dated people before this and I'd had long-term relationships, and I was fine, but when I started dating again there was a trigger.

I'd been in what I'd consider a toxic relationship previously, and there was a separate incident where I was sexually assaulted; with these two things I pinpointed why I think this all happened.

Thank you for sharing this with me; I'm so sorry you have had to go through that. I'm not a therapist, I'm asking this based on my own thoughts and feelings, but do you think that maybe in some ways the OCD became a self-sabotage, so that no one else could hurt you, and you could control the situation or be the one looking out for danger and controlling the narrative? Yeah, it's a hard thing. It's one of these things I've never actually been able to figure out because in my opinion, OCD interlinks with your self-esteem; it has for me anyway. I don't know what the science and psychology behind that is, and I also understand it's a genetic disorder. Maybe the situations I dealt with were the triggers, but it's always been a mystery to me as to why it started. When I was 13, OCD was not even something that was considered, but I had this really germophobic era, where I was constantly washing my hands and asking my mum for reassurance that I wasn't going to die because I'd touched something like a door handle, hadn't washed my hands afterwards, and then eaten some food.

I was really obsessed with it, but then it just went away. We put it down to some puberty anxiety because I was fine until I was 19 years old, which apparently is what often happens. I've done a lot of reading on OCD and how it manifests when you're a kid and then reappears in your adulthood.

I'm interested to know whether there is a correlation here. When you first started to have symptoms of OCD as a teenager,

had you started to understand you were attracted to guys, or thought you might be gay?

No, my experience with my sexuality is quite a weird one. I didn't know I was gay until I was gay. In hindsight, I knew I was, but it didn't click when I was younger. Just before my 18th birthday, someone I'm very close with came out to me. He said he was bisexual, and I said I thought I might be as well. As soon as he told me, it all just clicked in my head, and then the next week I went on a date with a guy.

I'm from a very religious family, and initially reactions weren't the greatest, but they're a lot better with it now.

If I'm being too personal, please tell me, but do you think that maybe this could have kicked off the OCD, in terms of self-sabotage because you didn't feel accepted when you came out to your parents?

Yeah, I think there's probably some aspect of that. I felt that my family were devastated by the news, but they were probably worried about me and not wanting me to catch HIV.

Wow, that's so common. I had the HIV comment in 2004 when I came out at 19. So, the fact that it's still happening, all these years later, blows my mind.

I wrote my dissertation on it. I wrote about the culturally traumatic effects of the AIDS crisis and how it continues to affect gay men today.

How would you describe your feelings when you were going through the loss of intimacy in terms of relationships and sexuality with yourself and with a partner?

I felt frustrated and very alien. I have explained it to so many people I've dated and people I've been intimate with, but they're never going to get it as it's just out of their frame of reference; they can try as hard as they can, but it always feels like this alien thing that I'm going through. It also makes me feel bad that my partners are really into me and wanting intimacy, and I'm freaking out. I feel as if I'm the problem, and OCD makes you feel that way too.

What I'd like people to understand is that this is constant. It's not that you have an hour feeling anxious about something, it's always in your head, there's no break from it. Any time I'd go socializing, I'd be having one conversation, but there'd still be this dialogue in my mind; it was always happening.

How did you manage when things were at their worst, and what support was there for you?
I've been very lucky with my support network in Cardiff. I have the most mentally aware, emotionally available friends anyone can ask for. I think that's partly on me as I'm very specific with picking my friends and making sure that they're empathetic people. Even when my mind is saying I'm a paedophile or something like that and my OCD is at its worst, I have a place where I can talk, and my friends will be there. I've gone through a lot of cognitive behavioural therapy (CBT) and exposure response prevention (ERP) therapy.

ERP therapy is the gold standard for OCD, where you basically put yourself in the situation. So, if I was having the thought, 'What if you're a paedophile?', I'd write down 'I am a paedophile', or if I was worried that I was going to break up with someone, I would write out a breakup text to my partner.

It's about embracing the things you're scared of. It's horrible, but it works.

I guess it's a self-acceptance. You're saying to yourself, I can't fight with this any more, and facing it head on, and so it loses its power. In my experience, fighting with the intrusive thought exacerbates it.
It's accepting that nothing is certain in life. You can never know anything for sure. Maybe there is a 0.1 per cent chance that I am my thoughts, but that's a battle I'm willing to lose.

How long was it from initially dealing with the OCD and it being at its worst, to getting to a much better place?
I think there's chapters within this. With the thoughts around relationships and not being into my partner or worrying about this, I hadn't made the connection that this was OCD, and I didn't know that OCD could even be that. Then there were the sexually intrusive thoughts, which pretty much ruined my life for about five months. I became suicidal and I self-harmed. I went to a Christian therapist, as I come from a religious background, and we just didn't know what was going on. I felt that the Christian therapist interpreted my thoughts as resisting temptation rather than being intrusive thoughts because she didn't appear to know what OCD was, and she didn't refer to the condition during our conversations. So, she started praying for me that I would be able to resist the urges I was having.

This traumatized me and was my first experience of therapy. I came away from that and googled how to get sectioned. I did not want this to be true and I never wanted to harm anyone. I was so scared that I was going to do something, but as soon as I searched Google, the OCD Action page came up with information about intrusive and sexually intrusive thoughts. I found a forum, with thousands of people going through the exact same thing. I remember breaking down crying, realizing this wasn't just me; it was such a great moment. After that, I got on medication, did a lot of therapy and I recovered quickly from that theme.

I went to Edinburgh to complete my master's, had a little break from dating, then came back to Cardiff and got into a relationship. I started dating someone that I really liked, and my mind was going crazy, but I was medicated. It was going reasonably well, and then he broke up with me, which was weirdly satisfying. It was a moment of realization that I could date, and to the point that someone else could break up with me. It was the first time I'd ever been broken up with and it was just a very freeing feeling.

Do you think it was freeing that it wasn't on you to make the relationship work, or to end it? Someone else can also end a relationship, and when this happens, and the fear is realized, what can you do?

Yes, it was a really empowering moment. Even though it sucked, because I really liked him, I went away from that with a new perspective on dating and an understanding that I could date. I dated another guy for about five months, but he wasn't ready for a relationship so that's why it ended. But before it all ended, for the first time ever, I hit a point of contentment with him. The intrusive thoughts had faded a lot, they were still there, but I was more in control of them. I did a lot of journalling at that time and wrote out my thoughts. When we did break up, it was afterwards that I understood what recovery was like. It was a realization that I had OCD for life, but how that affected me was a different thing. I have the tools now to show that I can get out of these spirals, and I can date.

How would you describe the time of understanding that you had this condition, which was affecting your ability to have relationships and meaningful intimacy, and trying to heal and move through that period?
A very insecure time. I'm sure there are external factors as well, which led to the insecurity I was feeling; I was chasing these relationships that I didn't really want, to feel connection, but also choosing people who were fucking me over constantly. I played it off as having terrible taste in men.

Do you think you were seeking what you thought you deserved at that point in time?
Yes, I just thought that I was never going to get into a relationship, and that was all I really could ever get, so I may as well make the most of it until I eventually reached 'gay death'.

Did you notice a change in your personality and your approach to day-to-day life during the time you were struggling with your OCD?
Yes. In my second year of university, I got into drugs and became very dependent on them. I wouldn't say addicted, but I was abusing drugs a lot, just a ridiculous amount of ketamine, Mandy and cocaine, at least four times a week for a year. My mental health was getting worse, and I was questioning why this was happening; it was obviously the drugs. It was

the self-sabotaging part of my life. To an extent, there's been a lot of self-sabotaging in my life, but this was an exceptional amount of it. I was self-sabotaging myself rather than just my relationships.

Do you remember a point when you started to feel a sense of acceptance about the situation you were dealing with, and considered how you would move forward?

During a drug binge, I had my first ever panic attack, which I interpreted as a heart attack. I didn't know what a panic attack was. I was taken away by an ambulance to hospital. This happened three times where I just called the ambulance because I was having bad chest pain, and after that I realized I needed to sort myself out. I went away and started to focus a bit more on my health. While I was at university, I still wanted to go out and get fucked up at times, but I moderated it and was mindful of how I was doing it, and made sure I was doing it for a good reason. Previously, it was just to avoid my problems because it was the only time I really felt normal. The only time I wasn't having intrusive thoughts was when I was high. I was able to express these feelings of love to people that I otherwise wouldn't be able to; I was able to communicate that openly to people I was dating when we used to go on nights out together.

What were COVID and lockdown like for you? Did that time affect your mental health?

COVID was such a blessing for my mental health. Obviously, a horrendous time for a lot of people, but I physically couldn't date. I always wanted to date, it wasn't that I lost the desire and I always tried, even though I knew it would fail because of my

OCD, but with COVID, I just couldn't put myself in that situation. It was a very reflective time of just being with my friends. It was what I needed to support the healing of my OCD.

Do you think during that time you became friends with yourself, and did it enable you to simply be with yourself and not run away from the issues you were dealing with?
Yes, it didn't cure everything, and I would say I've still got things to work through, but it was a reflective time to really think about who I was and what I was doing in my life.

You'd have been around 24 at that time. Do you think at that point, you'd started to see a new opportunity and a new way of living life? Do you think that it forced you to consider what was next for you, and get the support that you needed?
My OCD wasn't constant at this point; it was purely triggered by relationships. So, if I wasn't in a relationship, I was fine, and my mental health was pretty good. That extended period of not being in a relationship and not even entertaining dating was nice. After COVID, I made mistakes, but I was self-aware and I was working through things.

What did life feel like after you'd understood your OCD and you'd started to move forward with life?
The last few relationships I had were with men that I would consider emotionally unavailable, or certainly not what I would expect from a boyfriend, and one of those was with someone I thought I really liked. I was looking for commitment but they didn't want this from one person. I worked on myself for the first time ever and put myself in a head space of being either

single or looking for a relationship but no in-between. I didn't do the casual stuff. I'd had a lot of casual sex the previous year and it was coming from a very self-sabotaging place, but it wasn't related to my OCD for once.

What positive changes have you noticed in your life since making that decision?

I think I'm just a lot more mindful about my actions, and my friends' actions. It's made me a better friend too. I'm more invested in my friends rather than myself. It's fine to be invested in yourself, and you should be, but in a different way. It's work in progress, and I've got a long way to go, but having this self-awareness is important.

Do you feel that you've personally gained anything because of your experience of loss?

This is a hard question because, objectively, if I could take back ever having OCD, I would. This has been an awful time in my life and I would not wish OCD on anyone, but has it shaped me into the person I am today? Absolutely. It's made me a much more empathetic and understanding person and I think very resilient as well. I can handle a lot.

I've harnessed this situation into a lovely Instagram page, where I'm able to help lots of other people. It's made me very open, and I think that's the main thing, that I'm fully transparent and honest. I really wear my heart on my sleeve, and I think that's all because of this very traumatic thing that's happened to me and not wanting it to happen to anyone else. I'm refusing to let shame ever affect me again; I think shame is the biggest barrier for mental health. And that's why I started my mental health page in the first place, which has been such an integral part of my recovery.

Do you think, with all the understanding you have now, that your loss and the way you handled your loss was unique to you as a queer person, and that someone who isn't queer wouldn't necessarily have the same experience?

Maybe with overcoming the barriers of shame and commitment issues. I think a lot of it comes down to this heightened pressure in society to live in a very heteronormative, monogamous way, as if it's the gold standard, which I don't think applies to queer people, necessarily. If it works for you, great, but it shouldn't be the gold standard. I think at the same time, the feelings of loss in relationships caused by OCD aren't a queer experience necessarily. There are plenty of heterosexual people who are going through or have gone through it as well.

Why do you think it's important for people to open up about their experiences of loss?

Being open is the most freeing experience; there's nothing quite like it. Just knowing that I have nothing I'm hiding is such a weird feeling, and you can't quite describe it until you've done it. It can be very embarrassing when you first open up about things, but I've been this way for about two years now and it just makes things seem less important. All the big worries I have seem much more manageable. It's a freeing experience that I would recommend everyone to try.

Do you think your creativity has helped you, and has having your Instagram page felt as if you've taken your power back?

Yes. I have OCD, I may as well use it for good and make money from it. It's by no means something I can make a living from, but creativity has enabled me to make this horrendous mental illness into something that I can also take from. OCD took so much from me, so it is only fair I take a whole load back from it too.

Do you feel that the loss you've encountered in your life, as a result of your OCD, and the OCD itself, has supported you in becoming more resilient and equipped you to handle challenges as and when they're presented to you? If so, how?
Definitely. OCD is the worst experience I've ever gone through. I find it hard to believe anything will ever top that right now, until I'm proved wrong. I'm able to be resilient, and any other challenges that now come my way, I'm ready for. I got through it and it's as if nothing can be as bad as that, even another OCD spiral. I've always been very open in saying that I've recovered from OCD, but I don't know what's going to happen. I could have some traumatic things happen to me that send me on this horrendous spiral again, but I'm not afraid of that any more. I used to be terrified of that happening, but now I know that if it does, I can manage it, and I'll get through it again.

You have a toolkit now for what you need to do and how to support yourself. Do you feel as a queer person that understanding and exploring identity and sexuality, and your experience of living authentically, have enabled you to deal with these challenges in your life, in particular the loss you encountered because of your OCD?
Yes, absolutely. I think that my queerness is such an integral part of my life and how I live each day; I don't shy away from

it. I am very queer in my community and around my friends. There is still some toxic internalized homophobia that I hold, for example when I meet straight men, an instant deeper voice comes out, as a protection I guess, but as soon as I've realized they're fine, I turn up a bit! Outside that, I think it has just enhanced my experience, my human experience, and made me feel very blessed to be queer and special. I know there are shortcomings in the community because of long cultural traumas, and that we still have a lot to deal with, but I truly have faith in our community to be resilient and power through, as we have done many times before.

Do you think that your queerness was an inner resilience that helped you through a difficult time?
Yes, it's one of the things before the OCD that was probably the most insane thing I was going through – internalized homophobia and dealing with a world that didn't accept me. It set me up for and gave me the building blocks to become a resilient person.

What would be the one piece of advice you would give to someone experiencing any type of loss right now, or dealing with past events and trying to move forward with their life?
Just be kind to yourself. Recovery is not a constant. It's not linear, it's like climbing a mountain. Every time it feels as if you're taking a step back, just remember to look at how far you've already come and how much you've got through.

Do you believe in life after loss?
Absolutely. My OCD made me feel that love wasn't something I

was able to receive or give, and now I feel that I am deserving of love, and I do deserve to love people too.

Ask Silva

Is it more common for queer people to develop mental health conditions, such as OCD, than it would be for someone who doesn't identify within the queer community? If so, what support and intervention are available to enable the condition to be diagnosed and treated, preventing minimal impact to daily life, and in Zack's example, helping in situations like being intimate with a partner?

Studies show that queer people have more mental health difficulties than heterosexual people because of the on-going oppression and discrimination that they face, and a lack of specific support. Queer people often fall through the ever-widening cracks of the mental health care system because their specific needs are not being acknowledged.

Galop released a report in 2021 showing that 80 per cent of LGBTQ+ people using a LGBTQ+-specific mental health service were satisfied by the service they received compared to 38 per cent of satisfaction in the generic service. This goes to show that there is quite a big gap to fill in generic services to be better trained to meet the specific mental health needs of LGBTQ+ people.

We need more appropriate services for LGBTQ+ people. I believe that all healthcare professionals, including GPs, nurses, psychiatrists, psychologists and psychotherapists, as well as administrative and receptionist staff, should have thorough training in working with LGBTQ+ people. According to the Stonewall report, 13 per cent of LGBTQ+ people experienced unequal treatment from healthcare staff because they were LGBTQ+, rising to 32 per cent for trans people. This is unacceptable, but it also explains why some LGBTQ+ people may be reluctant to reach out to health professionals and therefore delay their care.

CHAPTER 3

Loss of a Parent

Euan

Age: 24
Pronouns: He/Him
Sexual orientation/identity: Queer
Occupation: Local government
Home town: Brighton, UK

Professionally, Euan works with families and young people with mental health difficulties, and in the fields of neurodiversity, risk management and safeguarding. Personally, he writes poetry, considers himself a board game enthusiast, a big advocate for sex positivity and queer as fuck!

In this interview, I speak with Euan about his experience of the loss of a parent. Please be aware that this interview makes references to poor mental health, self-harm, sex and suicide.

How do you tend to manage an ending or loss when it is presented to you?
My natural disposition is to shut things off and shut off my feelings; this is a learned behaviour through my past experiences. I naturally go to that place where I shut down and think to myself, *just get through this*, and when I am out the other end in a more consistent place, I might try and open the feelings and attempt to process and deal with things. Either that, or I will try and control the situation as much as possible. This is something that I am trying to learn to undo, and I am trying to feel my feelings a bit more around endings and be more honest about things, but it can be scary.

Can you share with me your personal experience of dealing with a loss in your life?
My biggest loss would be my dad passing. He took his own life when I was 12 years old.

Do you remember the initial moment you were told about this?
I was staying with my nan at the time, and she received a phone call saying that I needed to come home right away, and I didn't understand why. My stepdad came and picked me up; we were travelling in the car for about an hour and a half and during the whole car journey he didn't say anything. I gathered that something bad had happened and it was all going through my mind; had I done something wrong, had something happened within the family? I just didn't know what to expect and obviously my brain went to that place of thinking that maybe someone had died. So, I had this time during the journey to think and over-think, and this is probably where my issue with over-thinking started.

I got home and my mum sat me down and told me the news that my dad had passed away. I remember just crying; I didn't really understand at the time. I could feel myself crying, but this was before I had processed and could comprehend what had happened. We were both very emotional and had a hug which lasted for what felt like an hour. While I was very upset, I just couldn't make sense of it.

Do you think it was a natural body reaction because you had received the news, but what you had been told just didn't seem real?
Yes, absolutely, and as a kid I was a big crier, and I cried over many things, so it was just my natural default, but I couldn't fully process what had happened. I spent a long time in my room after that watching TV, slowly processing and coming to terms with the fact that my dad had died and I was never going to see him again.

Do you mind me asking if you know why he took his own life?
This is something I have had to investigate through the years. To be honest, I don't think at the time anyone really knew, and he didn't leave a note.

How did you deal with the loss and find understanding in what had happened?
It's tricky. I had a lot of feelings about what had happened, but I wasn't in a mature enough place to understand the feelings, let alone know how to try and deal with them. I think this is when my journey with poor mental health started, because I felt awful in myself, I felt angry, but I didn't realize how angry I felt at the time. I also felt sad and started to have these low

moods. I became very afraid of the world, of getting close to people, and I felt that I couldn't rely on anyone. I guess this was because the person I was supposed to depend on as a child had gone. I isolated myself, shut down all these feelings which then made it difficult to process them. I think this shutting down also came from trying to avoid making other people feel worse than they already did about the situation.

I remember distinctly going to his funeral, and like I said, I was a big crier as a kid; I felt emotional and knew I was going to cry. I remember going to my nan's house before the funeral, and I could tell instantly that when everyone looked at me they felt worse, because they would be thinking 'this poor boy', and I knew in my head that if I started crying it was just going to make people feel worse, and that was the last thing I wanted, so I forced myself not to cry. Of course, I did cry in the church, but then after the funeral I kept this attitude of 'don't be sad', 'don't cry', 'don't let anyone know you're feeling scared because it will make them feel worse'. I pushed everything down so much, but these feelings were all brewing inside me and would then come out in other ways.

I eventually realized that life just isn't worth living if you are shutting down your emotions, because you don't get the happy if you cannot acknowledge the pain. You either shut down all of your feelings, or you allow them all to be, and you accept that you get the good and the bad. I realized this around the age of 14 or 15 years old and recognized that I needed to start feeling things again, because if I did this, I might feel like a normal person again. I tried to make myself cry on many nights by watching sad videos or listening to sad music, but I just couldn't. I had drilled the blocking of emotions so deep within me, that I couldn't undo it, so it made it very difficult to process what had happened.

What strikes me is the awareness you had of what you were doing at this time and trying to make it better for yourself.
I didn't have many friends because I felt quite alienated, and I pushed everyone away. I spent a lot of time alone thinking, so I would over-think what was wrong with me, and I think this is why I am so into psychology now, because I had the time to think. I used to stay up at night, and at this time my mind was not in a good place, so I'd sit up and do mini therapy sessions with myself. I would sit in my bed and analyse what I was thinking and feeling, and then switch roles and think about what I might say to someone else in my situation if I was the therapist. This was quite intellectual, but it was also part of the problem for me. I could figure out what was going on and understand that my life was not good and that this wasn't how a person should be, but it didn't help me feel better. What I really needed was to feel the emotion and the pain I was in, in order to get through it.

What support was around you at that time?
I had supportive people in my life, but I found it difficult to connect emotionally. I had a role to play in this, because I had shut myself down completely, and I had distanced myself from everyone. It's funny because now that I work with children who are emotionally shut down, I can finally see it from the other perspective. I can do all the right things to support those children, but if they are emotionally shut down, it just won't make any difference. I did make a friend when I was around 14

years old. We got close as friends and I eventually opened up to them. I confided in them that I was self-harming.

Do you think the self-harming was a result of what you were going through?

My self-harming was more from the fact that I had shut all of my feelings down, but I needed to feel something; I had so much that was going on inside of me, but I just couldn't feel it.

Did you have an opportunity to speak with anyone to support you, be it friends, family or a professional?

I did speak to a therapist, but this was after I met this friend. This was a positive thing to come out of the friendship, as she gave me the idea and information to be able to get external support. I guess one of the issues was that I had already been over-thinking, having these conversations with myself, and acknowledging that something was wrong. I'd been completing research online as you do, trying to self-diagnose at 14 years old! In the end, I spoke to the counsellor at school and explained the situation and what was going on, and she referred me for external support where I was able to get CBT.

Going through a loss, you have the primary effect of the situation, but then you get the secondary effects as well. It's as if I feel shit, so maybe I am going to act out and argue with everyone, or be really sad and isolate myself from everyone. Then you have all of these relationship issues which are making you emotionally worse, that you need to deal with, before you can even deal with the bereavement and the reason you have been feeling like you have in the first place. It is a chain reaction that is complicated and messy, and can have such extreme effects, like families falling apart. It can be very difficult to navigate.

Something that really strikes me is the loss you had to deal with was only 12 years ago and you have come so far since then within your life. I cannot imagine what it must have been like for you at 12 years old, having to deal with this.

I hope that, in some way, you can look back and feel this and understand that the circumstances you found yourself in are not an everyday occurrence, it was happening at a time when your growth and who you were becoming as a person were influenced by such a life-changing situation. I have so much respect for you, your courage and where you are right now in your life.

Thank you. The time after his passing wasn't easy, and something that made it more difficult was that my nan passed away from cancer when I was 14 years old. I had a deep emotional connection with my nan; she was a nurturing type, and I was staying with her when I got the call to say I needed to go home because my dad had passed away. I used to go and stay with her for weeks at a time during the summer holidays, because we got along so well. You could tell she was a fucking ally too (of the queer community), she was so liberal, open and accepting, gave the most amazing hugs and was someone I needed in my life.

At the time when she passed away, I had shut my feelings down so much, that I wasn't even able to process the second loss. I was like an iron wall. At my nan's funeral, I started to laugh during the service. I now know that I often will laugh when I mean to cry; it's like a defence. I shoved my feelings down and wouldn't let them out, but my body wanted to cry, wanted to let it out in some way. I knew I couldn't do this, so the next best thing happened and I laughed to get something out at the very least. I later learned in life how connected your mind is to your body, and how emotions are connected also, and that trauma is stored throughout your body. There was so much inside me, it just needed to do something, even if it was inappropriate, just to get something out.

There is a brilliant book, *The Body Keeps the Score* (Van der Kolk, 2019), and it is all about how trauma is stored in the body and states that the traumatic memories you're going to store within you are based on how your body was at the time. I had EMDR therapy, which is all about feeling your physical sensations throughout your body and processing your traumatic memories. One example during this therapy was that I explored a different traumatic situation where I was crouching down in distress at a tube station in London, and during the therapy when I was processing this, I could feel my body moving into a crouching position from where I was sitting. I wasn't doing anything to make this happen, other than feeling my feelings. My body had stored this traumatic memory in my knees and legs, to the point where I relived and re-enacted the memory without even trying.

If you had to describe what life was like for you at that time, what would you say?
It was a confusing time, and I experienced it as if I was watching it all unfold and happen to someone else. I just really didn't understand and was constantly thinking about what would happen next. After someone passes, there is lots of preparation for the funeral, organizing flowers, all that kind of thing, but I didn't know what would happen after that was over. I had this untrusting feeling towards life; it was like if this can happen, something I never saw coming, what else could happen, what the fuck might come next? You need security at that age, and

the rug was pulled from under me. It was a time of terrifying anxiety, and life was just unpredictable.

What did life feel like to you when you started to process and deal with the loss of your dad?

There was a numbness at this time. I guess it was like being at the dentist, when you're having dental work, you've been given this drug and they are doing all these awful things in your mouth, and you just can't feel a thing – that is what I would compare it to. I knew there was a deep pain within me, but no matter how hard I tried, I just couldn't feel it. I had a lot of questions: why is this happening, why am I feeling this way? You're trying to rebuild your life but have no fucking clue how to do it. I had no clue how to create a life where I didn't have a dad. I think you embark on a misguided journey, where no one can give you advice and tell you how to do it, you're just on your way. It was and is tricky. You also make a lot of mistakes, and then you need to try and fix these, and continue this journey, and it feels as if it will never end. You question whether this is just how life will be from now on. Will it be in shambles forever?

The way I started to move on into healing was to give the 12-year-old me a big hug. I don't think I truly realized I needed this until I supported a young child who had lost a parent, in a very similar situation. I was giving him a hug to support him, and to meet the needs he had at that time, but coincidentally I think I was hugging myself at the same time.

What strikes me as significant is that at 12 years old, you don't really know yourself or understand that much about who you

are and who you will become, so when you go through a situation like this, how do you find yourself in a way that can help you move forward?

My goodness, this is the question of my life! I think about this a lot. I had such a drastic shift from being an emotional child, to then being a teenager who shut down his feelings. I guess I thought that to try and be me again was to be this emotional kid again. As I have grown older, I have had to rediscover how I am as an emotional person and change my narrative around what it means to be emotional, and what it means to be myself, and this has been a difficult and confusing journey. I think it was when I started engaging more with art, that I started processing my feelings. I remember distinctly starting my artistic journey through listening to Florence and the Machine, and music that made me sad, and eventually I could really start to feel emotions inside myself. I felt things that I truly didn't think were possible to feel, and then I felt encouraged to write, which then led to me writing a poem about my dad.

When I finished writing the poem and read it back, I felt fine for the first time, because my whole journey, and the bereavement I had experienced, was looking back at me on a Word document. It outlined the journey of feeling awful to feeling that I was going to be okay, and I knew that if I ever felt shit, scared or whatever, I could come back to this poem, I could read it and remind myself that I have been on a fucking journey, and I have arrived at the destination.

Was the poem your acceptance of the situation?
I think so.

Did you ever have a period of denial about what had happened?
Yeah, very early on when it first happened I had thoughts of it not being real and that it was a bad dream. I used to have these dreams about him, and it would be us spending the day together, and I also had a few where he said to me that it wasn't real, and that he had to disappear for a few years and now he was back, and we could continue. Waking up from those dreams and realizing nothing had changed, fucking hell, it was just heart-breaking. You have to live the whole thing over again; it was clearly my brain processing what had happened and giving me what I wanted – for it not to be real. I haven't had a dream like that in a very long time, and maybe this is because I have now finally processed the situation.

At what point did you start to feel optimistic, and that while you'd had to deal with such a difficult situation, you could see life moving forward in a more positive direction?
The poem was my acceptance and a realization that I was at a point where I was okay, but it doesn't feel like optimism. The very concept of optimism is a tricky one for me, and I have never really understood what it means to me personally. What I do know is that since my dad died, there was always something deep within me, a feeling of resilience that regardless of if I felt awful right at that moment or that nothing would get better, I could push on, get on with life, push down my feelings, and work hard, because it was just something that I needed to do. I knew I would find a way to get through it, to live, to tap into this resilience and intention when I needed to.

It is about survival. With resilience, it is about knowing I have the skills and the 'inner something' to get through what I need to at that time; whereas optimism is about thinking the future will be better, or that things will be better.

Optimism came to me through two very important friends in my life. I made friends with them when I turned 16, when I was not well and was voluntarily hospitalized for anxiety. I was discharged and had some time to relax, and I then started meeting up with an old group of friends, and they were part of that group, so this is where my friendship with them started. I was at a very low point, but they reached out to me. Before going into hospital, I texted this group saying that I wasn't well and would be going into hospital and would not have my phone with me; I didn't want them to think I was ignoring them. They arranged for a card to be sent to my home address, and it said something along the lines of, 'we don't know what is happening, but we want you to know that we are here for you', and this meant everything to me; I don't think they will ever realize how much. I met up with them not long after I got out of hospital, and that is when our friendship began and started to blossom. What also bonded us is that we were all going through something personally at that time, but we all brought out the light in each other, rather than the darkness, as had been the case with the friend I mentioned earlier.

We got jobs together, which was very funny. We would stay at one of their houses after we had finished work, and we would stay up until about 3am talking about our feelings, our fears, but importantly our hopes and dreams for the future. When I shared these things with them, they enhanced them rather than diminished them. I started to think it would be possible to have my dreams fulfilled and that I could move forward with life in a positive way, because I had people around me who were going to have my back and support me. I relied on them so much more than my family and we had the deepest conversations together. We discovered our sexual identities separately, but with the support of each other, and helped each other in situations we found ourselves in, because when the chips were down, we knew we would be there for each other, without question. I wouldn't be the person I am without them, and linking back to one of the themes of the book, we are all queer.

What positive changes have you noticed in your life as you have grown older and found a sense of acceptance in all that you have had to deal with?

Everything; I am a completely different person. I mean, I was a child and now I'm an adult, so naturally some of this is just down to growing up. I do feel that the experiences have made me strong, but I would like to break down this word. I thought I was being strong by shutting down my emotions and not letting them get to me, but now looking back and having gone through the entire journey, I realize that where I was then was weaker than where I was when I found out about my dad passing away and started on this personal journey. I now know that I am stronger, not because I can shut things away and deal with situations without crying, but because I can deal with any situation, cry, and feel my emotions.

I can deal with the situation that is presented to me and have feelings. Also, I have learned that I don't need to deal with everything on my own. I have solid connections with people around me, and I know I am going to be okay, because I can come to the people I love, even if I am not feeling okay, and they are going to help me to feel better. As a teenager, I thought I had become a very cold person because of what had happened, that I didn't care about other people, because in the end they might just let me down. I thought I didn't like or care about anything, to be honest. Now I work in care, I support others and through this, I have learned that all my previous feelings and lack of emotions helped me to develop an empathy that is so strong that it has enabled me to care about so much and so many people. I also used to think in a very black and white way; there was no room for the grey. Now I have come to love the grey area of life, because there are a million shades of grey to play around with, it is a beautiful thing to hold on to, especially when the chips are down. It may be a little grey today, but maybe tomorrow will be a little lighter.

Is there anything you look back on and would do differently in dealing with your loss?
No there isn't, because how it happened and how I dealt with it has got me to where I am in my life right now. I would just give that 12-year-old boy a big hug.

As difficult as this may be, given the circumstances we have been talking about, do you now look back at the situation with positivity, or a sense of gratitude and understanding, because of where you are in your life right now?
I am on my journey of loving myself, and I think my experiences play a part in this. I haven't completed my journey to loving myself, so I don't see myself entirely as being something I fully like. When I do reach this place, I might be able to look back at all I have been through with gratitude and appreciation,

but until I fully learn to love the person I have turned out to be, this cannot happen. I think, deep down, I still hold feelings of anger and sadness, but they're a million times less intense. There are times where I hear a song I know he would have loved, or I see a father figure in my life and think about what I could have had. I know I am stronger, and I am now able to help others, but sometimes I think about the fact that I would have liked to have grown up with a different experience, a less chaotic life and upbringing.

Do you still miss him?
Yeah, God, I miss him like hell. He was so lovely, he had his issues that he had to deal with, but he had a soul that was just incredible, and there are so many lives that he just lit up. I have learned a lot about him through other people now that he has gone, and it has reaffirmed everything I thought I already knew about him. I don't remember a lot of our 12 years together, but I have these preconceived notions about what he was like, and everything I thought is spot on, based on other people's experiences. Everyone says I look exactly like him; my mum says I act a lot like him too, and when I'm at my nan's (his mother), she'll be in the kitchen and I will be in the lounge watching the TV, I'll laugh at something, and she'll come in and say that it feels as if he's back. I wish I had him in my life because he sounded so great, but then I have to remember that I am him, an extension of him, and I am keeping his soul and legacy alive. I get to light up people's lives, just like he did.

This is the first time you have talked about the situation you have dealt with publicly, in the sense that this is being included

in a book about loss. I guess having known you for around a year now, I knew you had lost your dad, but this is the deepest conversation we have had about it. Do you feel comfortable sharing this generally with people around you?

I feel comfortable sharing much of my story with anyone, but I am conscious of how people will perceive it. Obviously, I don't want to go in, reveal everything so that this triggers someone else's experiences in life, so I don't go fully into everything but that is because I am more concerned about other people's feelings. I am totally comfortable talking about the experiences I've had, and this is because I have in my own way made my peace, or am on the journey to getting to that place. The few times where I do get emotional and feel the pain of what happened, I am then too emotional to go into it properly; 99 per cent of the time I am fine to talk about it, but that 1 per cent of the time I'm just not able to.

Do you feel as a queer person, that the experiences you went through helped with understanding and exploring your identity, sexuality and your experience of living authentically? It's evident that you had so much to deal with at such a young age, and life then threw this at you too. What was that like for you?

I was 15 when I came out. Through my childhood I had experiences where I thought, why am I really fascinated by this football player, for example. I didn't make much of it at the time. I realized I was gay through porn at around the age of 11 or 12, which I know is young. So even before my dad passed away, there was an indication that I was attracted to guys, but not to the point where I understood it; it was more fascination. I had an iPod touch, so no one knew I was looking at the porn.

I was 13 when I asked a girl out on a date, and I thought I was into her; it was nice because I like female company, but it was around that time I thought I might be bisexual. I wrote this down in some old diary, so there was an acceptance of queerness at some level, and I had a lot of time to myself to think.

I think deep down, I knew I had gone through so much by the time I came out, so what did it matter if I was attracted to guys?

What I find interesting is that you have gone through so much trauma at an age when you didn't truly know yourself, the most pivotal time building yourself up as a teenager, into adolescence and then adulthood.

How confusing was it for you to process the loss, but then for your hormones and sexuality to kick in? Did it feel like a burden, or was it a welcome release because it was a distraction from everything else you were going through?

In a way I think it was a distraction, and when I discovered my body, it became an escape, and provided a dopamine hit that I needed. I guess it was like a drug to lift me from a dark place. I loved an escape as a teenager; I was always reading fantasy novels, and I think maybe porn became this too. I was also lucky that YouTube had become a big thing, and there were lots of queer influencers. I would stay up all night listening to all these people's stories – it was a godsend, so incredible. The reason I love being gay, queer and everything that comes with our community is because when I realized I was gay and part of this community, it was the first time as a teenager that I wanted to find and be myself again. I'd finally found something about my life that wasn't awful. I fell in love with everything I learned about the queer community, because it was a light that I could go towards. It was an opportunity to reinvent myself and find who I was. I discovered nice traits about myself, like fashion, feeling good in my clothes and how I presented myself.

Do you think being queer saved you?
Absolutely.

I think about my generation and the experiences of people I know, and I don't think this would be something I would commonly expect to hear, especially growing up in the 1980s and 90s, so this is just beautiful. Of what you've experienced so far, what has been the most meaningful or valuable lesson you have learned?
To feel. This is the advice I would give to someone else – don't shut things down, it is not the way we are meant to be. As painful and as horrible as it can be, you will reach a better and healthier place by feeling and processing your emotions.

Finally, do you believe in life after loss?
I believe in a better life after loss, I really do. I had to discover my chosen family and identity to really believe in life after loss, rather than just surviving. There is a real difference in this.

Ask Silva

Can experiences of loss at an early age in life support queer people in coming to terms with their sexuality and/or gender identity, because they are more aware of

difficult emotions, and may be experienced in how to process these?

Queer people often feel different from a young age, even before puberty. This is because we are socialized so early on with heteronormative and cisnormative stories and ideas. Some of us may experience difficult losses and grieve deeply, such as losing a parent. Many of us will have lost a pet as the first experience of grief. But, for queer people, there is also a loss and grief that is not often acknowledged: the loss of childhood for spending much of it trying to hide who we really are as a protection against rejection.

Society only provides a heterosexual 'model of life', so, early on, queer people understand, either consciously or unconsciously, that we do not fit with that model, and we have to make our own path. It can be freeing, but also very scary. Queer people tend to develop more awareness of their sexual and erotic processes and their gender expressions because they do not fit with 'the norm' and therefore they pay more attention to them. Feeling 'different' can give us the opportunity to understand our sexuality and gender identities in greater depth than heterosexual people.

Family Tree
WRITTEN BY EUAN

I am my father's son,
And the apple does not fall far,
Similar in colour and complexion,
Yet also rotten to the core.

Mutated seed, a poisonous tree,
Grown in ethanol-stained soil,
An apple like this stands no chance,
Causing itself to decompile.

But do apples always fall,
along the same path?
Soil can be tended with help,
Upon another's behalf.

Though his apple may decompose,
It fuels me with growth,
And I can grow and be happy,
Happy for us both.

CHAPTER 4

Loss of Safety

Jamie Windust

Age: 26
Pronouns: They/Them
Sexual orientation/identity: Queer and non-binary
Occupation: Contributing Editor at *Gay Times* and author
Home town: Dorchester, Dorset, UK

Jamie Windust is an award-winning writer and is currently Contributing Editor at Gay Times. *Their debut book* In Their Shoes: Navigating Non-Binary Life *was published in 2020 by Jessica Kingsley Publishers and was longlisted for the 2021 Polari First Book Prize. As a storyteller, Jamie uses their social media presence alongside their skills as a writer with the aim to provide compassion, humour and awareness to those who need it.*

In this interview, I speak with Jamie about their experience of loss of safety in society as a queer person. Please be aware that this interview makes references to bullying, hate crimes, poor mental health and transphobia.

How do you tend to manage loss when it is presented?
I think there is a perceived lack of control for me as a queer person. So, a lot of the time when it comes to things ending – like friendships, relationships and work relationships – I like to be in control of how they end. I think as an adult, I can understand why I find it important to have that control, because as a young queer person when I experienced the endings of friendships or rejection, it felt harder to control. A lot of it was a rejection of me as a queer person, and it was something that I couldn't control at all. When I manage endings now, it's important for me to be able to feel as if I have the control and space to have my say in when things end, rather than feeling that they end because they're my fault.

We are talking about loss of safety in society as a queer person. How would you describe the loss you have experienced personally?
It's an interesting concept and much like prejudice in all its forms, I don't think I realized that I had a loss of safety until it was presented to me via prejudicial treatment or violence. So, it's a slow burn as an adult. I've slowly realized that that is something that is true and painful. There's a grieving process when it comes to understanding that there is a loss of safety as a queer person and a lot of that is out of our control. It's hard because although we can regain a sense of safety as queer

people in small ways via community or allyship and having supportive allies who can help us feel safe, I think there is a frustration and a sadness that encapsulates this feeling of a lack of safety because of the way society is set up. Structurally, we are a group that is marginalized so it can sometimes feel like two steps forward and one step back, because of this wider understanding that we aren't as privileged as our heterosexual or cisgender counterparts.

When did you understand this was a loss you had experienced, and how old were you?
I was probably around 10 or 11 when I realized that I really loved dance, so it was something that I did a lot of. That was the first time I experienced this kind of rejection because of the idea that dance wasn't something that was allowed. It wasn't seen as something that I should be doing. It felt like a rejection of my desire for joy. Essentially, I just wanted to have fun and there was a rejection of this and then bullying as a result and this idea that it wasn't necessarily safe to fulfil or act in accordance with one's desires or interests.

It's interesting, because there wasn't really a huge stark moment where I realized, but it was just a process of learning that I wasn't as safe as my peers, or there were things that I couldn't do that they could quite easily do without a fear of safety. There was a gradual feeling of loss and of opportunity – up to this day.

How did you deal with the loss, and find understanding in what had happened?
This wasn't necessarily a loss of a person or a specific relationship

but more, if anything, a loss of a relationship with myself. I don't think I fully understood what was going on until quite recently. So, the understanding that I was almost grieving myself and grieving a life that I wasn't able to live safely has only really come into the forefront of my experience now. In the past, I was unable to understand what was going on and I didn't have the means to experience it in a way that felt comfortable. I remember feeling quite angry a lot of the time, acting out with alcohol or sex or just feeling as if there wasn't a means to express myself in a safe way. I don't think I did ever process it at the time; it was something that came later.

What support was around you at that time? Do you recall a particular moment when you felt seen and supported?
As I got older I had more of a support network with fellow queer people at university, but didn't really have that experience of huge levels of support. There were more conversations happening at the time at school around LGBTQ+ people, but we were only a few years outside Section 28 being repealed, so it wasn't as open or communicative as we see nowadays.

I did have one instance where someone noticed that I was very angry because of being bullied. I could tell that they could see this anger and this frustration in me, and they could see that I wasn't happy. It turned out that this person was also queer, and they came out to me. That was an affirmative moment because it was someone seeing me without me having to make myself vulnerable. Because I didn't want to make myself vulnerable due to the fear of being rejected, it was nice for someone to see between the lines, to see me for me, identify with me, make me feel reassured, and also make me feel it was okay to feel angry.

Can you describe what life was like for you during this time?
This period of feeling unsafe and realizing that my days of feeling unimpacted by the world around me were slowly dwindling was quite sad. It was that naive childhood energy of just wanting things to be fun and to play and have a good time which made it a little bit more insidious, because I didn't really understand what was going on yet. The world around me had already decided that I was queer and I was at fault and was to be treated differently, despite me not having put the pieces together myself yet. I ended up leaving dancing and not exploring what my hobbies or desires could even be. Now, as an adult, it feels as if I'm giving myself that permission again to be more open, to find out what I like doing, without giving into the fear that I'm going to be rejected and subsequently lose everything around me.

Did you notice a change in yourself, your personality and approach to day-to-day life during this time, and can you describe what this looked and felt like?
Once I understood that the world wasn't necessarily as safe for me as it could be for other people, there was an inherent frustration and anger that manifested within my experience. I became quite rebellious, not necessarily being as kind as I could be to others, ignoring rules and feeding into that dynamic of rebellion. It was like, if you're going to reject me, then I'll make it dramatic and something that is not necessarily pleasant. At

the time, I don't think I was aware of what I was going through, so I wasn't always conscious of it.

It was almost as if I knew I was being rejected by others, so I rejected myself at the same time. I lost my perceived sense of safety and my sense of self completely.

I felt angry and frustrated and that stayed with me for the best part of a decade. It was such a formative time as well, finding my sexual identity and my gender expression. It felt that a lot of that was perhaps clouded by the rejection and the anger and frustration that I held on to. I don't see that expression of myself as inauthentic, however. It wasn't necessarily coming from a place of love, compassion or kindness to myself, it was coming out as a middle finger to the rest of the world.

What emotions were presented to you at that time, and do you remember feeling a sense of confusion and denial about what was going on?

There definitely was a sense of confusion. I was confused as to why this happened to queer people, and there was a feeling that we can't always necessarily access the same safety that other non-queer people can. I was just frustrated with the whole experience. I do remember feeling this real anger at not being able to change the status quo myself, and having to accept it, and that felt hard because I didn't want to accept it.

How long did this go on for, and do you remember the point when you started to feel an acceptance of the situation? What did this look and feel like for you?

I think I accepted it quite quickly because the evidence was obvious to me that this was true. So, seeing continual hate crime, receiving a continual amount of prejudice on the streets, I was able to understand quite quickly that I'd lost my sense of safety in the world. I did, however, really struggle to accept that it could be my experience for the rest of my life; this was a fear that I held.

At what point did you start to feel optimistic, could see life moving forward, whether that be acceptance of the situation, new opportunities or a new way of living your life?

That was quite recently. There was more of a sense of optimism when I started therapy and was able to understand that a lot of this shame and fear that I was holding was being placed on me by the world. It wasn't something that I had to carry, although it felt as if it was mine to carry. I felt as if it was on my shoulders to try and work out how to stop queer people being targeted. Once I realized that it wasn't *just* my responsibility, it was a collective responsibility of society, and it wasn't my fault that this was happening, I was able to feel more optimistic. I felt optimistic that I would be able to regain some of the safety that I thought I'd lost, and it wasn't all completely gone. I was able to understand that a lot of this is to do with perception of the world, and I was able to acknowledge that in my life around four years ago.

What did this new phase of your life look and feel like to you after you had processed and dealt with your experiences of the loss?

A lot of my new beginnings started after I joined recovery, started going to therapy, and it felt like a weight being lifted. There was a sense that this was a community struggle, and an acknowledgement that not everything was awful. There were things in the world for queer people that were blossoming, and I just learned how to navigate the world in a way that wasn't pessimistic, or put myself in situations where I felt trapped or unsafe. I was able to put boundaries in with the world, with my work and with friends and family. That made me feel more comfortable with acknowledging that I was safe and I hadn't lost everything.

What positive changes have you noticed in your life since understanding and processing your loss?

I'm a lot kinder, and I think that's important. I've become kinder to others and to myself, and I'm able to have boundaries with myself and my work which I've never had before and which have been influential. I'm in an era of changing my perception on the world; not necessarily changing myself too much but being able to acknowledge what I need to change and also what I can't change, and therefore what I need to let go of trying to control.

Do you feel that you have personally gained anything, because of this experience of loss?

I've gained a better understanding of myself, and of my community. I also understand my limits. It's important to understand that I am a very sensitive person and I can't do a lot of things, but that doesn't mean that I'm limited in any way. It's great to be able to say, I don't think I can do this, or I need more help in being able to do this, rather than just ploughing in and thinking I should be able to do this. I've learned to not live my life in 'should have' or 'would have' statements, but instead just give myself time and space to understand when I need more help and how to ask for it.

Is there anything you look back on and would do differently to support the internal processing of your loss, and to move forward with life?

I'd look back on this idea that it wasn't my fault. I do still feel sad that there wasn't enough support for me out there, and I feel a lot of queer people right now don't have enough support to understand that the things that are happening to them aren't their fault. We live in a world where we like to blame, and it can be really validating and easy to blame other people a lot of the time, and sometimes that is important. But equally, I think queer people will often just take a lot of the shame and a lot of the blame that they don't need to. So, looking back, there should have been more support for me, and other queer people like me. I hope now that there is more help for other people, and moving forward, I'd like to try and help other people realize that they don't have to hold on to that shame or blame.

As difficult as this may be, do you now look back at the situation with positivity, or a sense of gratitude and understanding, because of where you are in your life right now? For example, would you be the person you are today if you hadn't experienced the loss?

I do have a sense of gratitude; however, I don't think that that is necessarily something people should always instantly gravitate to. We live in a society, especially with social media, where if we see pain, we think we instantly must get over it and use it to our advantage. That takes time, and it must come naturally and organically. I can now look back with gratitude that I was able to seek help when I needed to and unlearn a lot of the things I had learned.

Do you think with all the understanding you have now, that your loss and the way you handled your loss was unique to you as a queer person, and that someone who isn't queer wouldn't necessarily have the same experience?

It was 100 per cent unique to my queerness, my transness, and that was why it was so difficult, and why a lot of these approaches must be unique.

How important is it for people to be open about experiences of loss?

We often lose a lot in our lives whether that be material things, physical people, or in my case here, a sense of safety. It's important for people to talk about that because in my experience, a lot of it is often perceived rather than actual, so it can feel as if you lose things when you don't, or you can think you've lost everything when you haven't. It's important to talk things out because you can speak with other queer people and understand that all is not lost, and everything is never lost. There's always a way to come back and find things that you may have thought you'd never find again.

Is this the first time you have talked about the situation you have dealt with publicly? If so, why do you feel comfortable talking about this now?

I think it is the first time I've spoken predominantly about this loss and, again, it's quite an organic feeling to talk about it. For me, there's an instinct of wanting to help others through the work that I'm doing now, and as a writer and as a person with this experience, to be able to help other people is fulfilling. It's a good time to share because I am now living a life that I thought had been lost to me as a young person – a life that didn't seem accessible at all.

Do you feel that the loss you have encountered in your life has supported you in becoming more resilient, and equipped you to handle challenges as and when they are presented?
I don't think that should be the predominant thing you should think of. If you are experiencing loss right now, it's great to want to feel resilient and to aspire to feeling resilient, knowing that it can make you stronger, but equally it's important to acknowledge when we have lost things in life and to just appreciate that this can be sad. It is important to hold space for that grief and that sadness, and not think there is a need to be strong, or a need to get through what you're going through. Letting yourself be soft and gentle is an incredibly important part of the process.

Do you feel as a queer person that understanding and exploring your identity and sexuality, and your experience of living authentically, have enabled you to deal with the challenges of life, in particular change and loss, as and when they arise? If so, why is this?
They have enabled me to handle rejection a lot better, so I'm able to see that things aren't as black and white as yes or no, especially being a non-binary person. I don't live my life in this or that, or black and white, so I'm able to see rejection, things

not going to plan, things getting lost or people leaving my life with a lot more softness and a lot more compassion towards myself than I used to. For me, originally thinking I was going to lose everything because of being queer, that has put me in quite a strong place to be able to handle lots of very different kinds of loss within my life and know that I will get through whatever is presented, no matter what.

What has been the most meaningful or valuable lesson you have learned?
Self-compassion, because without that I wouldn't be able to understand that loss is something that I can get over. It would just consume me, so without self-compassion, I wouldn't be able to know that there is a future after loss.

What would be the one piece of advice you would give to someone experiencing loss right now, or dealing with past events and trying to move forward with their life?
There's no one way that you should be handling loss, but I think it's important to speak to people. In my experience in recovery or in therapy, being able to hear other people's experiences of loss, no matter how different they are from mine, and understand that we have a similar connection and we understand even if the context is completely different, has been really important.

Finally, do you believe in life after loss? If you do, how long did it take you to feel this way?
I do believe in life after loss, and I think it is important that no matter what's going on, whether it be the loss of loved ones,

loss of identity, loss of self, loss of a feeling of safety, that you do feel this. In my case, I know that there is a future but it took me 10–15 years to be able to understand that. There is a future after loss, there is life after loss for us, and we never know what it's going to look like, so we need to stick around to find out.

Ask Silva

Safety and a sense of belonging are vital for queer people, but as Jamie has experienced, this isn't always possible. Can you explain why finding this is so important?

Safety and a sense of belonging is very important for a queer person because the world is not always safe for us due to homophobia, biphobia and transphobia. We have to be careful where we go, who we interact with and what we do in most spaces that are not queer ones. We have to scan for threats. Even in a country like the UK that is deemed 'liberal', homophobia, biphobia and transphobia are rife, both overt and covert.

Having safety and a sense of belonging is a place of respite for us, a place where we can plugin to our amazing queer energy and keep going. It is also a place of queer joy. Those queer places are special because they are not readily available to us everywhere in this heteronormative world, but they are essential for our good mental health.

CHAPTER. 5

Loss of a Previous Life

Juno Roche

Age: 59
Pronouns: They/Them
Sexual orientation/identity: Fluid
Occupation: Creative
Home town: Las Pocicas, Spain

Juno Roche was born in the 1960s into a working-class family. School was a respite, but shortly after beginning their university course, Juno was diagnosed with HIV, which was then a death sentence.

Juno is a survivor; they outlived their diagnosis, got a degree, and became an artist. But however hard you try to take the kid out of the family, some scars go too deep; trying to run from AIDS and their childhood threw Juno into dark years of serious drug addiction, often financed by sex work.

Running from home eventually took Juno across the sea to a tiny village in Spain, surrounded by mountains. Only once they found a quiet little house with an olive tree in the garden did Juno start to wonder if they had run too far, and whether they have really been searching for a family all along.

In this interview, I speak with Juno about their experience of loss of a previous life. Please be aware that this interview makes references to abuse, drug abuse, homophobia, sex, sex work, transphobia and violence.

Was there a loss in respect of your previous life, following your transition, and did you grieve for that life, even though you were living authentically as you?

Yes, but it's complex and nuanced because in a way you could say, before I transitioned, like wholly transitioned, because I've been transitioning, my whole life, I'd been trying to move out of the identity I was given to something else. Before I transitioned, I was a drug addict for most of my formative years and engaged in criminal behaviour, trying to earn money. I was selling sex, I was doing any number of things to get by and I was on drugs, injecting drugs especially. There's a kind of real harm there, there's a harm that you do to your body. There's a sense of not feeling and wanting to feel.

Part of the thing for me about being trans was I couldn't inhabit my body, so I couldn't feel anything. I would inject and still not feel anything; I wanted to feel something, and I wanted to feel real. I would end up in terrible situations, like crack dens in East London, or in Egypt, having smuggled drugs there. When I transitioned, the madness stopped, because I could feel myself suddenly, I was in this body and I was here, and I suppose I then distanced myself from that life.

I see that old person almost as a husk, like a shell that I discarded, and weirdly, the older I've got, the more I've seen the past as skills, life lessons, kind of adventures. Without all those adventures, I couldn't have done what I've done now, I couldn't have moved to a different country on my own. I didn't know anyone here, and I've got no partner or children. I live in the middle of this tiny village in the mountains, and I couldn't do that had it not been for all of those adventures that I had in a way, because your body is like a landscape, and all those years I spent pummelling my body with drugs and being in endless risky situations have enabled me to inhabit a new landscape.

Do you think you were self-sabotaging, or putting yourself in risky situations, because you weren't living a truly authentic life that you wanted?
Absolutely. I never wanted to die, I always wanted to live. I've always been optimistic. I don't like that glass half empty because I always feel as if I get it wrong. I've always been an optimistic person; I wake up in the morning and I see a blue sky and think, it is a new day. That's just the way I've always been. In a way, I wanted to destroy this body because it didn't fit me.

So, the loss was there from birth, would you agree?
From the get-go. I was born with a body that really didn't work for me. It was beyond working for me, and I didn't understand it. It was as if I was in a different country to my own country; I didn't understand the way my body walked, I didn't understand how people received my body, I didn't understand how the

world talked to me. I would see people use my old name and it was as if I could see it come towards me and then just fall on the ground. I would think, must I pick that name up, because it just doesn't land on me, it doesn't land when people say he. In fact, no genders ever landed on me. You know, maybe there's a kind of fluidity to my gender, maybe if I'd been born 20 or 30 years later, I might have just found it much easier to identify as being non-binary.

I was born into this body, this skin, and this skin is something which you have an intimacy with, you can't not be intimate with your skin. You know, simple things like you need to clean it, you need to look after it, you need to moisturize it, you need to wash your hair, you need to do this stuff to keep your skin working. You can't just decide to ignore your body and ignore your skin. But doing drugs and doing them for that long was a way of doing that. I was a heroin and crack cocaine user at best. I mean, I'd do anything, and I'm laughing about it now, but it's not funny. It was a terribly sad way to live. I woke up and ten years had gone.

I think that being on drugs was a way of trying to get rid of the loss. In all that time, I would be selling drugs, on drugs, selling my body, but I'd also applied to university. I went through it, I did a whole degree as a drug addict and I was on heroin from start to finish, so I was still positive.

There's obviously a part of you that wanted more for your life, and wanted to live an authentic life. It sounds as if you were held back by the shackles of being identified as the wrong gender. Then the drugs were keeping you back as well because you were lost in that respect. Would you agree?

Well, the drugs became an excuse. The drugs became the reason why I was there. When I was younger, I really wanted to learn, to be at school and learn, and I was the only one out of my siblings that finished school; the rest were excluded.

I completed exams, O-levels as they were then, and A-levels, and I would come home and say, look, I've got O-levels, and no one would say anything. I'm not saying that for self-pity, but it was just a truism of my life. So, then I had to make education, I had to try and find the value in education myself because there was no one around me saying this is important, do well at school and you can become this.

If someone had said that, then in a way my body might not have felt so desperately uncomfortable, but my body felt uncomfortable in a house that felt the same. I mean, I love my family to bits, but I felt like a stranger. I really like classical music, I like reading books, I liked my teachers, I wanted to make art; in a way there was a loss of education because there was no celebration of any of that.

I'm 60 this year. I look back over my life and I've written and published four books, I've been on radio, podcasts and television. I've been interviewed by Lord Grey, Head of the BBC, so much stuff, but I've done that in a kind of solo way. My family know that I write books, but I don't think that they know the extent of anything I do really. I don't blame them for that, as they have a completely different life to me, and I think partially there's this thing around being working class. People feel that the way to solve the working-class issue, if there is a working-class issue, is to take a working-class person and drop them into Oxford. I went and I talked to Oxford University, Cambridge University and the University of St Andrews. I've been invited, paid and put up to talk to all of them, and I go there and can't believe it is real. I'm dumbstruck by the kind of glory and beauty of it, and I could never have got to those places because I had to struggle to get to school the next day. So, there's a loss there in terms of the fact that everything was much more of a struggle and a fight.

I've said this before, and I don't mean it to sound glib, and I certainly don't mean it as a recipe for anyone or a suggestion for anyone, but for me drugs were a relief. There was a relief to being utterly smashed, and I chased that, which is why it lasted for as long as it did, because I just wanted relief from my body not feeling right. I'm not going to say it's the wrong body because I've got a lovely body. I love my body, so it's not about being in exactly the right body, but it's the way the world interpreted my body.

How old were you when you started to realize that maybe you were not in the wrong body, but that you didn't identify with who you'd been born as?
I was around eight years old. In the playground at primary school, the boys used to call me Pansy, but I really liked the name, so I got everyone in the school to call me Pansy because I knew it fitted. For the first time, I thought they may be calling me it thinking they were hurting me, but I was thanking them. My book *Gender Explorers* opens with that story; I literally loved being called it, so I asked everyone to call me Pansy, and that went very wrong. I mean, in 1972, that didn't go well, and then I knew.

Before I transitioned, I didn't ever identify as gay, but the gay scene was somewhere that I felt very safe within. I was diagnosed with HIV in the very early 1990s and, in a way, the gay scene was the only place that was providing any kind of support and kindness. But I never really identified as being gay.

I've got great friends from that time, and I got to be part of the most brilliant, marginalized community. I got to dance in the 1980s in great nightclubs; I loved dancing, I loved having fun, and there was no better place to be at 4am. I loved dressing up and costumes, and I lived in a big house in Camden, a big squat with drag queens and models. And you know, it wasn't all bad, that's what I'm trying to say.

You transitioned later in life to live authentically, but before that you blocked out your feelings with drugs, not feeling like you fitted in the world. How would you describe that time?
Yeah, I think I probably did. So, two things. One, I think it's important to say that there's a wholeness to me now. In my last book, *A Working-Class Family Ages Badly* (Roche, 2022), there is a picture of me as a five-year-old on the back, and I've never changed my birth certificate. There's this kind of notion of having a gender recognition certificate, and I've never wanted one. For me, it was important to try and remain kind of whole really. So, the person I was born is the person that is still within me, and I feel as if I'm a good caretaker of that person now. I feel that I look after them well.

For a long time, I was angry and often people who do drugs, people who inject drugs, are like that. I was angry at feeling so disconnected from everything. If you'd been talking to me 20 years ago, there'd be a real disconnect and loss with who I am. But you're talking to me at 60, and I've done a lot of work, especially since being in Spain. I've done a lot of work to forgive, a lot of therapy, a lot of therapeutic stuff with myself too, like walking, exercise, diet and yoga; writing has helped too. I've done all those things to try and mend that fractured self, which I think can happen with drugs.

Do you think creativity is healing?

Creativity, queer creativity and trans creativity. It's no surprise to me that the best books, the best exhibitions, the best everything that's coming into this world now come from a place of queerness and transness.

I'm saved by creativity; I always had it, and we downplay it because we say, you must be successful, you must have a career. Write some articles, write a long article, write a book, write whatever. The nice thing is that somehow, with all of that messed up, fucked-up life, I'm in a really privileged situation now where I have this space and time to be creative. I look back at the five-year-old me and we've got the same bags under our eyes, our life was always heavy. I know that person is still part of me, but I look after them in a different way now. I care take them and I make sure they're okay.

A lot of people have said to me that I should do the gender recognition certificate, especially because I'm living in Spain, because it could come up as an issue. I don't want to, because when I die, I want it to say that I was born this, and I died this, and there was no clarity. The truth of transness – and maybe queerness as well – is that it's a completely brave act, brave state, and a creative state too. You must believe in stuff that you don't know is going to exist yet. You must think, I can be this person and this person could feel more comfortable. Contrary to popular belief, it's not about being beautiful or sexy or this or that. It's just about feeling spacious and comfortable.

So, I think creativity and transness go hand in hand. When people say, 'I'm sorry you've got HIV and you're trans', I think, why? I'm sorry that you haven't got it. You'd be more interesting if you did, you'd be smarter, you'd be more empathic towards other people, you'd care much more about the wars around the world. I'm really blessed. I'm blessed by two things in my life: by being trans and by being creative; those two things are all the bravery I needed to do what I do now, and to have the life that I have. Listen, if you'd have said to me when I was 30 and I was on drugs and for rent via a cheap little advert in the back of a magazine, out of a flat in Euston with my friend, you will own outright a beautiful house in Spain, in the mountains, I would have said fuck off, I'll be dead.

I find your book *A Working-Class Family Ages Badly* and your story so inspiring, and I think it's inspiring to anyone who reads it for a few reasons. It's the way you identify as trans and talk about transness; there are people within the media or within the public who say things that are inappropriate, say the wrong thing, or don't care what they say, and that's just not okay. Then there is another kind of extreme, where everyone's a bit afraid of speaking and getting something wrong.

What you're doing here, and how you just described transness, is that it's not a one-size-fits-all approach. How you define your transness might be completely different from how someone else does, but that's the beauty of it. We get to all be who we are, have that freedom and it releases the binaries that society has created.

All transness is doing is loosening stuff. You know, the world is fucking falling apart. Falling apart because of the way that we made it. We chose to make it in this ridiculously narrow way based on capitalism, on gender binary, on good and bad, good being a heterosexual relationship with two children, and bad being everything else. We based building a whole world on slim pickings, and those slim pickings would be amassed by a few people. Transness is a loosening of the shackles that bind us. That's all it is. I'm not being poetic, I'm just being honest.

I was part of that shackling because I thought I was going to have surgery, and after surgery, I would open my legs and just be a woman, but that wasn't what happened. What happened was that I just felt trans. I felt trans and I felt ultimately queer, and queer in the most anarchic way. I felt that I wanted to ask better questions and better questions of my body. I didn't want to have this thing that my body is either feminine or masculine, or this or that. I didn't want those kinds of questions because they feel so dull and stupid. I wanted to ask questions like, can I explore, and can I explore the world in more than one way? And I have done that. I love this part of Spain; I love the sunrises and sunsets, I'm obsessed with it. The embodiment of my transness is this house in the middle of the Andalusian mountains. I make art, write and do whatever I want to. I owe no one anything; I'm not beholden to anyone, and there's a kind of beauty to that, and that's privileged, I get that. I'm completely privileged, but I wasn't born into it; I've had to really find my way to it.

The other thing that's inspiring is your journey. I don't mean to sound patronizing, but your book is so raw and honest, and there are so many moments where it could have gone horribly wrong, but here you are celebrating 60 years, and in a place of feeling your best self.

Yeah, but honestly, it could have all gone wrong. There were bad times in crack houses or drug houses or when I robbed dealers. When I was diagnosed with HIV, before effective medication was available, loads of people died, loads of people I knew, my friends, people I loved. We talked about the gay community, and loads of people who were part of my family from that community died back then. I did nothing different, there's no bravery. There was no, 'I fought it like a battle', none of that shit. I was doing heroin, so I was far from that. It's a kind of gift that I'm here, and I'm going to put it down to my trans goddesses, who looked over me and kept an eye on me.

I think one thing we talk about after loss is that in-between stage, before we find the new beginning or whatever that might be. The mid-part of your life was about drugs and living a life that you weren't entirely happy with, and you were surviving and just doing what you needed to do to get by. Do you remember your thoughts and feelings during that time, and do you remember thinking about a new life or trying to make one for yourself?
I don't remember a lot of it because I was literally out of my skull most of the time. What I would say, and I wrote about this in my book, is that in the very thick of all of it, maybe five years into addiction, all you do is drugs, you do nothing else. You get money to do drugs, and that goes on 24 hours a day.

You don't really sleep because you can't, and because you need to use at four in the morning. There was a time in my life where someone told me they would like to treat me, and I could go anywhere in the world. I chose Egypt. I suppose my request is the type of request which you may say defines me as a person; I said I wanted to go and see the Valley of the Kings, and I wanted to see the Nile. I could have said anything really. I could have said I wanted to go down to Selfridges, get some clothes, or something expensive, but I wanted to go to Egypt. It was absurd because we had to smuggle drugs into Egypt, and it all went hideously wrong. That's the central point of my book, *A Working-Class Family Ages Badly*, that it all went wrong, but even then, there was a part of me that knew I'd be back.

We didn't leave the hotel room. We got to the hotel room, started to do drugs, closed the curtains, and just did drugs for four days until they ran out, and then we were chased out of the country. I knew I'd be back, and I remember driving to the airport, stopping at every pharmacy, as we found out that you could buy Valium over the counter at that point in time in Egypt. So, we bought all the Valium we could possibly buy, and then were just literally stuffing them.

I remember looking out of the window of the taxi and seeing all these signs for things like Karnak Temple, Luxor Temple, Luxor Museum, the Valley of the Kings. I think that I had a kind of pragmatism. I knew I wasn't going to stop doing drugs then, I was leaving Egypt to go to Hackney to get a £20 deal. That's how tied into it I was, but I knew I'd be back. I remember then daydreaming about Egypt and becoming obsessed with it, becoming obsessed with the history of it. I was reading, finding out about the country, making drawings of stuff, and saying to people that I'd been to Egypt and here was a drawing of the pyramids. I hadn't seen anything but there it was. I believed in it so much that I knew I'd make it present in my life in some way or another.

I went from having a completely dead mind, which in a way was the in-between space, a kind of almost not dead, but a deadening space, to having this sense of wanting to do stuff, to explore the world over the wall. I'd had that feeling as a kid, too. There was a world over the wall where a father wasn't violent. There was a world over there where it happened differently. I had to believe in that, because if I didn't, then this was all I'd got, and that couldn't be it. I always had this thing in my head, which is why I think I'm here.

I'm making art now, which I've not done for 30 years. A friend of mine said to me the other day, 'What do you think you're doing?' And I told them, I'm going to have an exhibition, because I believe that I will have an exhibition. And not because I'm arrogant or anything at all, but because I just believe in the greatness of the world. I believe in this world, even though it is in a bit of a two and eight at the moment.

Yeah, but you've put so much out there already that's come to fruition. Why not? You know, why can't you have an exhibition? I'm committed to and protective over trans youth and young people, because I believe in a world for them. I believe that this world can be brilliant, although it's a bit screwed now because of the systems that we've set up. I wasn't given a choice; I was born into a situation that was tough. I then created other situations that were tough because I just mirrored what I knew. I didn't know a loving situation, so how was I going to create a loving relationship? I only had relationships in the very early days with people who would hit me, because that's what I knew.

I guess we look for what we feel we deserve. Yeah, and you feel comfortable with it. When someone would say, I love you, I'd ask, what the absolute fuck are you talking about? I didn't know what that word meant. I mean, it's taken me years to understand that, and to get to this place where I love me, my life and what I've done, and where I'm proud of myself. It's taken years to be able to say that.

When you made the decision to transition, what was this experience like for you, and did you face any barriers during this time?

Transitioning took quite a long time. Transitioning, as in a medical transition, was a different thing because when I first tried to do it, because I was HIV positive, no one would do it, and it was considered elective surgery. I couldn't even get a dentist for years because of my HIV status. I still have a fear about this, and I've lost teeth at the top of my mouth.

I hate what I was put through at the dentist, as someone who lived with and had an AIDS diagnosis in the early 1990s. Also, because of what was happening to gay men, queer people and drug addicts around that time, they were being treated terribly by anyone who was scared that they would have AIDS or HIV.

People said AIDS in the early days; they didn't say HIV until later.

The medical transitioning took quite a long time, but after Egypt, I knew I couldn't do it any more. It took maybe until my early forties to really put my life back together again, but I'd started to take hormones in my late thirties. I was taking hormones but then changing my mind, because I didn't really know how to do it. I wasn't born into a place that was going to teach me the skills to do big things like transitioning, so, I had to learn that the hard way, and I did. Some people do it brilliantly and with such an elegance, and I'm in awe of them. When I say elegance, I mean in terms of structurally elegant, rather than being elegant as a person, but I was all over the place, and I was living with HIV.

HIV has been a defining thing in my life, because when I was diagnosed, there were headlines that said things like, 'Ship them off to an island and shoot them', and that was almost every day, not an occasional thing. So, I came through those times, and to a certain extent, I had an inbuilt fear of healthcare professionals asking me questions and telling me that I had risky blood. I had learned to sweep up after myself to make sure that there were no traces of me left in a room. We've all seen the conversations all the way through the 1980s and early 90s, saying it should be a criminal offence if you recklessly or intentionally pass on the virus, but I don't think anyone, or very few people, has ever intentionally passed HIV on.

Most people interact with other people because they want to have fun, love or they want to be held. They want to be touched, and none of that stuff is about intentionally wanting to harm, it's about wanting to be human and have connection and contact. It took me a bit longer to get on top of all that stuff, structurally because of HIV, but in my head, I was a completely different person.

What were the feelings going on at that time for you internally?
It's taken me until now to understand those feelings. I'm 60 this year; I came to Spain at 50, and it's taken me all this time, but I get me so well now. I've written four books, and those four books were about an exploration of all the stuff I have experienced; some of that was me, and some of that was the stuff around me, like class, sex, sexuality, gender and addiction.

So, it's taken me a long time to get to this place and it's utterly different to where I was in my early forties. I can finally breathe. I don't have to get up, and I don't have to go out and do my drugs. You know, I realized that I was bright, that I could become a teacher. I think I started training as a teacher very early on into my recovery, at around 39 to 40 years old.

I love your honesty. Your life and the stories you tell, although some of them are different, remind me of Maya Angelou's – the courage to live a full and unapologetic life, full of adventure, trials, tribulations, with such a rawness to them. Have you read her books?
Yeah, I really like them. I've got them here, where I've got my go-to set of books.

I can't claim to feel like I'm in the same space as someone like Maya Angelou, who is just in a goddess realm, but I think that there was always a belief in me. There was a belief in me that something existed over the wall and that I had the creative capacity to make that become real. I still walk around this house, not every day now because I've been here for a long time, but I think, this is it, I've done it. I've got the wisteria in the courtyard, which frames the door and hangs down in this great purple haze.

Before we started this interview, you talked about the year you'd had. So, there's a part of you that kind of relates to this belief and what I am talking about, otherwise you wouldn't be writing this book, and doing the other stuff that you do. A part of you believes that there's got to be more, and you need to find out what it is.

Some of us do it through talking, writing or making art. I always had the belief despite all the stuff I experienced, so when I look back at it, I think it looks and feels like a film in a way. Why wouldn't the lowest be as low as the highest was high? Why wouldn't that be the case? What I've learned to do over the years is to mellow out and find a place in the mid-ground, where the creativity can be all those things.

I love what you said about your age, and how you've processed the experiences of your earlier life, in later life. I think there is a need or want for us all to have everything figured out. I had therapy in the summer and ended up discussing a situation that happened when I was in my twenties, which I thought was finished business, but it really wasn't. The loss that I felt at that time was still lingering in my body, because the emotion was still there. Maybe this stuff never really leaves us, it just shapes us and helps us move forward to become the best version of ourselves.

I agree, and it's a bit like a sculpture or something that you would pare back; you're constantly moving towards a better understanding of who you are, but you'll never get there because you will change during that process. I'm not scared of dying because of HIV and AIDS; I have no fear of death and I love getting older. Sometimes people say to me that their best years are behind them, and I tell them I don't want to listen to that. I think that my best years are still in front of me, even if it's only six months.

I feel as if my best life is still here, and I don't care about getting older or looking older, getting lines, or grey hair. I don't give a shit about any of that stuff.

It's unimportant, because I lost friends who died of AIDS, and they died awful deaths in their mid-twenties. So, for them,

I don't give a fuck about the lines on my face, it's a complete privilege and we are really spoiled. If we think we're that important that we need to keep this one mug of ours looking young, then we are as much of the problem in a world that has bigger problems. We internalize all of that, think we're that important, and that we must keep being beautiful. Fuck off! Not that many people want to sleep with me any more because I'm getting older, and I don't care because, you know what? My life is about the mountains and creativity.

Frankly, I put all of this down to my mum, who has never feared getting older. My mum has lived her life to her fullest. It's really damaging if you're scared of getting old, because you put a kind of false ceiling in the room and think, well everything must be sorted out by this point because no one's going to want me. Of course, at one point not so many people are going to want you, but it doesn't matter because you should want you more. If you allow yourself, you're going to want you more, and you're going to want the truth of you, and the best of you, to be the thing that drives you.

Do you think that, with all the understanding you have now around your losses and the way life has been, your experiences were unique to you as a queer person, and that someone else who isn't queer wouldn't necessarily have the same experience? There are certain things that being marginalized and othered by society enable us to slip out. We're seeing it more and more. The world is essentially a very broken model, that's why we have people like Trump and Johnson. There are these broken models where governments are having to pay people's electricity bills because they're so high. I live in a country that has a socialist government, so it has a different system, and I get to see first-hand here how my body is central to this government's policy making. What queerness does is gives you a chance to get out of that and go to a different land, even if that is nightclubs in Soho or Brighton, or Pride celebrations or even at the other extent of that, chemsex parties.

Listen, I'm not saying those things are good or bad. I make no judgement because I've been a junkie, but what I'm saying is that we get to inhabit different realms. I think that's part of the beauty of being queer, and somebody like me is just essentially an old-fashioned, slightly anarchic socialist who also believes in a more radical way.

The saddest thing for me is when queerness becomes more like them. I really don't want to be more like them. When people say to me, do you think you're a real woman, I just think of the fucking stupidness of saying that. We make up this stuff. None of it's real. You know, we invent this stuff, money isn't real. We give it all reason, purpose and fictions, and then we must believe in the fictions. So, no, I really like my stitched up, changed, upcycled body! I believe in the brokenness coming together. I've incorporated my losses into the sins of my body. So, the losses have become integral to me. I can't walk, run or hide from them; you must take them, look after them and carry them around with you.

Why do you think it's important for people to open up about their experiences of loss?
It's power, and it's empowering. I know that there's a thing around the word power, but we must feel like powerful beings; not powerful in a way of firing a rocket like, you know,

the leader of North Korea or whoever. That's not power, that's something different. That's a lack of power, it's fear.

We must feel powerful in our own skin because we're only going to live and tread these footsteps once. So, talking about stuff and bringing it to the fore is important. I've had great talking therapy over the years, which I think is a must, and when I started being a teacher, every school had a counsellor who kids could go and talk to. It was a brilliant thing. The Tory government has taken away most of that and said, it's not important. What's important is the map, the piece of the pizza, league tables and maths, and it's just bollocks. Who needs to know the surface area of a triangle? What we need to know is that we're not bad people, that we're going to learn how to do the best that we can. We do that by talking about our sadness, our losses and by working out how there's a strength in all those things.

I look back and I think, what would I have done if I had started everything in my life earlier? I started writing books late, so I've dealt with ageism throughout my whole career, because of starting everything later. When I was writing for magazines, I was writing alongside people who were in their twenties, and I was in my early fifties. They would sometimes write things, and I'd think, I haven't got a fucking clue what they're talking about. I left the club scene in the 90s for example; I've got no concept beyond that, and no desire to know anything more.

Even sadness can become a strength and maybe that's what I've done in my writing. I think that's why people like my writing. When I wrote about Egypt, I wrote as much about being white, and how my whiteness had led me to believe that I could go to Egypt as a junkie and it would be all right. I could go and stay in a top hotel in Egypt and my whiteness would mean it was all okay. I think all of it must be on the table. You must reflect and think, I've done this badly. That was really privileged, to think I could go there as this white junkie and have an experience in a hotel that people had paid good money for. I went on a boat trip, and I was sick over everyone because I was coming down from heroin. How dare I think I could do that? I think living a good life is being able to incorporate all that stuff and not run away from it, not run away from the sadness, the loss, or the violent encounters, or whatever it is. It is about incorporating all of it and knowing it all makes up me.

Authenticity is power, isn't it?
Absolutely. I don't want anyone any more; I don't want a relationship. I will meet people and I'll say, I don't want a relationship, you know, you seem lovely, you seem ideal and funny, but I don't want a person in this house with me now in this part of my life. There's a sadness for me with that, because it would be lovely, but I know it wouldn't serve me well. What serves me well now is this, the mountains, the sunrises and sunsets.

Do you feel that as a queer person, understanding and exploring your identity, sexuality and your experience of living authentically have enabled you to deal with the most challenging situations around loss or in life generally, and if so, how?
I think it's that thing that, as queer people, we've had to find answers elsewhere. I remember when I was first diagnosed and I was given a piece of paper which said essentially I had six months to live. I had signed a piece of paper that entitled

me to death benefits, and because I got these death benefits, I could go and have all these alternative treatments I'd never had before. So, I had acupuncture, for example, because there was no medical treatment at that time.

I feel blessed, but also, I feel terrible saying that because people died. For me, it was something that taught me a lesson, because I thought I was going to die, and there was no medicine that could help, but someone would rub my feet, stick needles in me and give me acupuncture, or provide sound therapy. I remember thinking I was lucky to have this opportunity before I died, because I'd never had this.

For a long time, queer people couldn't get married, couldn't get any kind of insurance, all these things we were shut out of. If you were HIV positive, you couldn't do anything at all, so you had to become inventive. You had to look elsewhere to resolve the kind of difficulties, and the rejection, because this place that you don't want to be rejected from is rejecting you anyway.

There'll be some queer people who don't experience this, but most queer people, even in the act of coming out, will have experienced the fear of being rejected by this thing that calls itself the right way of being, and somehow having to fit in. In that process, we often find other places; we talk about our created families, invented families and our friendship families. We have all these things that we build up. I think anyone who is marginalized by the centre of the world, you know, it looks an awful lot like Carrie and Big, in *Sex and the City*, that's why he gets called Big, because he's a mountain at the centre of a very collapsible, stupid world.

I was interested in writing about that. I never did because I just thought, you know, that's the truth of that whole stupid fucking series. Years of *Sex and the City*, just completely based around the central thing of all that's wrong with this world.

I think that queer people look elsewhere, and that's often why when people outside the community are looking for solutions to their problems, they look to us. You know, back in the 1980s and 90s, every woman thought they should have a gay friend because they will solve their problems, or we could rescue them. I'm not interested in rescuing them. I'm not interested, as a trans person, I've never been interested in being accepted in their group because, frankly, their group is fucking broken. So, if you want the term real woman, have it. Because what I'm going to have is broken, in Andalusia, and happy.

That's the perfect way to end the interview. I love that. Do you believe in life after loss? And if so, how long did it take you to feel that way?

Yes, I've always believed in life after loss because I've always believed there was a life over the wall. I've always believed there was a different world, but I just couldn't see it, I couldn't smell it, I couldn't draw it. Well, I did try and draw it, maybe that's what my art always was, maybe that's what my art is about now, about me trying to capture this part of Spain.

However much those fucked up men in Silicon Valley talk about living forever, we should really stop, we shouldn't listen to any of that shit, because this world can't afford for everyone to live forever. What an egotistical thing to think that your life is that important. Just do the best you can do while you're alive and don't hurt anyone. This is all we've got, but if you're going to get stuck in loss, then that's your life. There are some people spending their whole life unhappy, sad and not being able to get over something, but I still believe that the best is yet to come. I believe I will have an exhibition, and I believe I will see the trees in my garden get gnarly and old – that to me is the best that is yet to come.

Ask Silva

As we have read through Juno's experiences, growing up and throughout our lives, understanding and accepting who we are as queer people can be difficult and extremely complex to navigate. How does a parent supporting their child, if they are aware of their queerness, aid the growth and development of the child's mental stability and security? How do they enable the child to face and manage their differences when they become aware of them, and as they move forward throughout their lives?

This is a very complicated question, but I can only provide the simplest of answers: love. When parents bring a child into this world, they have to let go of their own expectations, stories and dreams, because those things are theirs, not their child's. They have to fully accept that their child may have any sexual or gender identities, and they may develop in ways that may appear strange to their parents, and yet, the parents have to continue to hold and love that child, even beyond their own understanding, and help their child develop with their own stories, not the parents'.

Of course, it is hard to be a parent because they have to let go of so much in order to provide a truly genuine space for the child. When there is a warm, loving and caring space in the family household where the child is free to develop as they need to, the child will be more likely to turn to their parents when there is a problem such as bullying at school, or questions about accessing porn, or sexual health. Many children avoid having those conversations with their parents for fear of reprimand.

CHAPTER 6

Loss of Community

Vaneet Mehta

Age: 31
Pronouns: He/Him
Sexual orientation/identity: Bisexual
Occupation: Software engineer and published author
Home town: London, UK

Vaneet Mehta is an Indian bisexual man born and raised in Southall, West London. He is a software engineer, writer and public speaker and the founder of #BisexualMenExist, which went viral in 2020. He has appeared on numerous panels and delivered talks to various companies. He has written for Men's Health, Stonewall *and* Metro UK *and his work has been published in* The Bi-ble: New Testimonials. *He is the author of* Bisexual Men Exist *and the co-editor of* It Ain't Over Til the Bisexual Speaks.

In this interview, I speak with Vaneet about his experience of a loss of cultural and bisexual communities. Please be aware that this interview makes references to biphobia, homophobia, poor mental health, racism and suicide.

How do you tend to manage losses or endings when they're presented to you?

I don't think I'm great with loss. I feel the thing I often struggle with when it comes to loss is lack of closure. I used to feel like that when I stopped talking to a friend or something like that, and I always felt that there would be this moment of closure; you would have a discussion, you would understand each other, you would clear the air, so to speak, and you would move on. I realized that closure was a lie and it doesn't happen like that. It's not like it looks like in movies or TV, and it's like that when it comes to community as well. You fall out of it, and you don't really get to have a moment where you go to that community and say this is how you made me feel, and for them to address that and confirm they understand you and hear you.

I think the other thing is that the pain never really fades. It gets lessened, it reduces, but never really fades. The impact of it hurts a little bit less but sometimes it will come back up and you'll have a moment where you reflect and realize it kind of sucked. It's just about how you manage those lingering feelings for the longer term.

We're talking about loss of community as part of your interview; can you provide me with an overview of those experiences for you?

My first real loss of community was my South Asian community.

I grew up in Southall in West London, which is an area popu-
lated with Indian people, Pakistani people, and people from
the South Asian area. The high street has Indian food shops,
Indian clothing shops, sweet shops and restaurants. My school
was representative of the area. As I got older, I felt as if I was
doing things that were outside this community. I guess I felt
I was drifting further and further away from the constructs
within our community of what it means to be a man, what it
means to be South Asian.

I felt as if there was a backlash that I was getting for drifting
away from it. It was something that never unsettled me when I
was in primary school, but as I got into high school and as I got
older, I wasn't really blossoming into the man I was supposed
to be. I was failing in certain areas. I didn't speak the language,
I wasn't into cultural traditions like the music or the movies,
and people were asking, 'Are you sure you're even part of this
community?', 'Why don't you do or like any of this stuff?' Then,
I critiqued part of the community, and people didn't like that
either. I questioned why the woman was always a damsel in
distress in the movies. Why was it always set up like this? Why
was she even with this awful guy? People were asking, 'What
is your problem?'

Back then, I didn't really realize that was, in its own way,
queerness. It was me not liking the status quo and wanting
to change it, and people didn't want me to do that. It was me
wanting to indulge in my community but also indulge in things
that sat outside it too, and people didn't really like that either. I
remember having a bust up with someone, who didn't like the
fact that I wanted to put on Christmas music during Christmas,
as they wanted me to put on Bhangra music. They called me

a coconut, which means brown on the outside, white on the inside. That was the sort of thing that I dealt with a lot. I found it quite difficult, and I felt that as I was receiving that backlash, I had to let my community go.

I thought that if they didn't want me as I am to be part of this, then I didn't want any part of it either. I felt as if I almost had to shove it away and not even indulge because people were saying I wasn't enough.

When it comes to the LGBTQ+ community, this was difficult on two fronts: the bisexual front and being a person of colour, because even though I shunned parts of my community, I found myself a space with other people who also felt as if they were ostracized in some way. I still had friends who were South Asian who also felt they weren't part of this community, and there were ways that we spoke about things, which didn't necessarily sit right within the LGBTQ+ community because of how white the community was. So, with me speaking about cultural appropriation, speaking about and making jokes that white people do this, and white people act like this, people got very offended. I felt that I couldn't have these conversations in this space because people didn't welcome them and thought of it as a personal attack rather than a commentary on the differences in our community.

For me, the bisexual issue was realizing that the community was very gay dominated, and gay orientated, which meant that when I was talking about things that sat outside this norm, about what it meant to be queer, what it meant to be gay, people would ask why I was there. It took me so long to find acceptance within myself and feel as if I needed a community, it almost felt that I lost something I never really gained. I felt that the LGBTQ+ community would be there to support me, but

I realized that it wouldn't very quickly, and understood that I needed to maybe go somewhere else.

I did find other spaces. I found the bi community, I found a person of colour community, a queer person of colour community, and I found some sanctity within those, but dealing with those losses and realizing that there were spaces that didn't necessarily want or need me was quite a hard thing to deal with.

It sounds as if there are three losses that you experienced. Can we talk about the South Asian community first? How old were you when you started to think that you didn't fit in there?
I was probably around 13 or 14 years old, during the early years of high school. I realized that I didn't fit in with the other guys, and therefore, didn't feel like I fitted in at all.

At that point in time, had you started to explore your sexuality and understand that you may be bi?
I started to have feelings that I was bi, but I didn't explore them because I was already experiencing this backlash, and I felt that if I then put that out there it would just be another nail in the coffin. I experienced homophobia before I ever came out, because people already pinned me as outside the norm of what it means to be a man, and they said I was gay. I said I was not gay, but inside I thought I might be, although I wasn't going to tell them that.

I feel that I purposely shoved that to one side and thought I couldn't explore it because it could mean what I thought it meant, and if it did, then I would never be accepted.

It would mean you'd be rejected from your cultural community?
Yeah, and I wouldn't have anywhere to go.

How long was it before you then came out?

I didn't come out until I was 25 years old. It took me a long time, and I think the difficult thing for me was not knowing where the community was, and specifically the bi community, because for a long time, I didn't know bi existed. I didn't know bi existed until I was 18 years old, and when I found that out, I also discovered that no one believed it existed. People said it was a word that some people use, but it was fake, and they were making it up, or they were just doing it for attention. As I got older, I started to meet people who were openly gay and proud of their identity, but I never met anyone who was bi. I tell a lie, I did, but everyone ridiculed her. So, I thought, well, maybe that's not a real thing. I never met a bi man, so for a long time I thought that wasn't something I could be as I wasn't seeing it in the media, and I wasn't seeing a community. There's a lot to be said about the fact that the bi community doesn't have that same platform, and that means that bi people feel less able to come out because they don't see themselves reflected.

You decided to step away from your South Asian community, but was there something about not wanting to be completely rejected by your community for coming out as bi in the future?

At the point I came out, I was no longer connected to my cultural community. My family had moved out of Southall when I was 21. I had also moved out because I went to the University of Nottingham, so I had already left the community in terms of its place. I know that the South Asian community is much bigger than just Southall, but for me, that was where it was and that was my specific part of that community. So, there wasn't the fear of losing that community because it had already been lost at that point.

When you did come out, how were your family? Were you accepted and what was your reality?

It was difficult. My siblings were accepting, but my parents, not so much. They weren't outright rejecting. When I tell people how my parents reacted, they always think it's quite bad, but that's kind of the best I thought I would get. So, I feel that I did well. When I came out to my mum, she was shocked, and I was worried that she would hate me. I asked her if she hated me, and she said, no, but that she wasn't happy. That was honestly the best I could ask for; I thought, okay, I'm not dead to you. At the time, I wasn't really speaking to my dad and when my mum told him, he said that he was just concerned that everyone else would find out.

For me, it was like my parents didn't want me like this, and that was difficult to deal with, but I felt that was going to happen. My biggest fear was them kicking me out of the house, or if they told me I was dead to them or didn't want to see me again. I didn't think my parents would be that severe, but there was a part of me that wasn't sure because I knew they weren't the most accepting of queerness. They had made comments in the past and weren't that accepting. I was concerned about what would happen, and their reaction was honestly the best I could expect.

I'm so sorry you had to go through all of that. It's hard because there's so much to contend with, when coming out generally, but when you have different elements to deal with in terms of where you fit in the community, your cultural community, and parental relationships, it makes everything so much more complex to deal with. I'm interested to know whether you were disappointed in the queer community when you were trying to find your place, first as a bisexual person, but also as

a person of colour. You mentioned the bi community not being very visible, or people making biphobic comments. Were you disappointed by the community?

I was. I found it hard to deal with because I only finally came out because I could no longer deny my attraction. For a long time, I was trying to deny my attraction, but I fell in love with someone I was close to, and I then questioned whether I could deny this any more.

I finally did come out and a lot of things happened with this person, not directly related to my sexuality, but I found out that they were talking behind my back. I then fell out with other friends and lost a lot of friendships that year. They didn't directly say it, but I feel it was me coming out that triggered this process.

When I was stepping into the queer community, it wasn't even just about finding a community again, it was finding friendship again; it was finding people to talk to because I didn't have any friends. I wasn't close to my extended family, or my immediate family. Being around them was distressing because although my parents didn't hate me, it still wasn't great. So, finding that network, finding chosen family, finding people to be close to was what I wanted, and it was difficult because there were people who I thought were nice, and then I would bring up a conversation about race and they would reveal their true colours. Or I would bring up my bisexuality and you could just tell by their reaction sometimes, that they didn't believe it existed.

I was in a community called London Gaymers, and I was having a conversation with another bi person in the group; they were talking about feeling like a 'bad bi' because they had more sex with one gender than another gender. I told them I hadn't had sex with this gender, and a gay man listening in questioned how I knew I was bi. They should have known it doesn't work like that. There were also interactions with me having to fight against bi-erasure where people say that a celebrity was gay, and I would need to challenge and say that they were bi. So many conversations like that happen in the community, and not just the stereotypical ones, such as someone telling me I wasn't bi and I was just gay, which I did get a lot. Too many assumptions are made, like you're feminine, therefore you're a bottom, which just isn't the case.

I'm glad you're sharing your story, because I think that it sheds a light on what it's like not only to be a person of colour, but also to be a bi person in our community. In trying to belong and find your people, you're not just contending with sexuality, you're contending with so much more than that. You've then got the background of culture and parental relationships, and it must be really challenging when you put all of that into the equation. How would you describe your feelings around that time? From my interpretation of things, there was a lot to contend with in quick succession.

I first came out in 2017, and I didn't enter the queer community until the end of that year. It was 2018 and 2019 when I started finding the problems in the community. I realized that there were spaces I couldn't be in any more. I stopped attending London Gaymers so much, and stopped talking in it as much because I was dealing with those conversations and I'm one of those people who if someone says something that I feel is out of line, I'm going to call them out on it, and there are a lot of people who don't like that. Some people don't do that, so they're not used to it when others do it. I deal with it a lot in my own family, where people think I'm the problem because I'm the one calling things out. Someone in my family will say something incredibly racist and I tell them that it's not okay, and everyone will say I'm the problem for creating a drama. I challenge this and say it's not okay. We agree on that, but it's a case of, let's not have the conversation. I say, no, we should have the conversation.

I dealt with similar situations a lot in the communities that I first started joining, and then realized those spaces weren't for me. I saw some people outside those spaces, and made friends, but I needed to find something else. I started finding other bi people, other queer people of colour and interacting with them, going to some of those spaces, but again, finding some other issues like realizing the bi community was also very white, and that the queer people of colour community was still very gay dominated. So, I tried to navigate all of that, realizing I just needed to find people and then maybe spend time with them outside those spaces and build my own community, where I could have a party and invite all those people I'd met from the different parts of my life: my own space and my own community.

In honesty, I find it difficult to resolve, because sometimes I look at all of this stuff and I understand that it's made me who I am – but also that no one should have to go through that.

Did you have people around you who could support you at that time, and people you could reach out to and express how you were feeling?

I had a couple of close friends left and I spoke to them a lot about what I was dealing with, and also people I'd met in the community. We made group chats on WhatsApp and had conversations, and that was what really got me through a lot of this stuff, finding and realizing these were my people, these were the people who would be there for me.

It was the same thing when I felt ostracized in high school. I found the other people who were also ostracized, understood that these were my people, and we hung out – that's what really got me through. It is about understanding that I may not have 'the community', but this is my community, this is my chosen family and these are the people who will be there for me.

The concept of chosen family is so important; finding and making your own family. Was there a change in your personality or approach to day-to-day life when you understood everything that was going on, and what you had to contend with as a bisexual person of colour?

Growing up, and even to this day, I have a lot of anger. I'm someone who's quick to anger anyway, but a lot of the stuff that I was going through made me generally an angry person, and some part of that still exists within me. There's a lot of anger at the world and the way it is, and the things I've had to deal with.

Sometimes people in my life will say something, and I become angry, I guess because baggage still exists. These scars exist because of my experiences. I've managed to work on and try to heal them, but they're still there. They've faded, maybe been rubbed over, and other things have patched over them; they've got plasters and band-aids, but they're never completely gone.

These are part of what made me an angry person, and it's

only as I have worked through that stuff that I feel I've maybe come out the other side, where I still have some of the anger, but I've found ways to reconnect to who I was, and who I am as a person. If anyone had described me when I was young, they would have said that I was a very smiley person. There are photos of me with the biggest grin on my face, when I was seven, eight, nine years old. I was someone who used to pose a lot. Part of me understands that that's who I am, that's who I was, but the anger is still there, and that can be fuelled in other ways, rather than being the core part of my personality, as it was for maybe a decade of my life.

In recent years, I've been finding ways to connect to parts of my culture. So, when I talk about my cultural community, I connect with it through food. I love our food, our art, the textiles, the figures and all the symbolism. I like connecting to it in that way, the spirituality of it. I find ways to connect with it of my own accord and realize that now that I'm on the outside of it all, my community is what I make it, and my culture is what I decide it's going to be.

I'm connecting with it in a way that I enjoy, rather than a way that is dictated by someone else. It's the same thing with the queer community; this is what it means to be queer for me, and so I'm going to interact with it in the way I want to. I don't love *RuPaul's Drag Race*, but I love drag, so I'm going to go and watch drag and enjoy it in my own way. I'm going to dress queerly in the way that I enjoy dressing queerly, rather than the way that I feel is often dictated by the queer community. There's nothing wrong with any of that, but I'm going to dress like this, and I'm going to grow my hair out longer, wear earrings and that kind of clothing, rather than what is dictated by anyone else.

Whether it's culture or the queer community, we sometimes think we need to aspire to be something but when you can do that on your own terms, that's powerful. We don't want everyone to look, be or act the same; the diversity of everything is so important. While you're still angry about certain things, there is also a sense of acceptance in terms of where you are right now, how you're managing your life and your interactions with your different communities. How long do you think it took for you to start to feel this way?

It took a while, and 2017 and 2018 were rocky years. Frustratingly, it was only as we were moving towards the end of 2019 that I really felt I was finding myself. I thought 2020 was going to be my year, and then we know what happened with COVID. That is why I sometimes lament, even mourn, that time a little, because there was so much that could have happened, in respect of finding myself, and I was almost set back a few years. I was connecting to parts of my community that I was happy with, on the precipice of being part of something and really feeling comfortable in it too and then I lost it all again.

That period also gave me a lot of time to digest what had been happening. I found my partner during COVID, so it gave me that. I moved out of home, because I was living with my parents, and that really gave me the opportunity to become myself. I wasn't holding myself back living at home, but moving out also gave me new ways to find myself.

When we bought our place, I could buy the artwork and the furniture I wanted and make the place my own. Obviously, I had to consult with my partner, but in some regards, I could decide what existed in my house, what my house would look like, what went up on the walls, what colour the walls were, for example, and I was able to put myself into everything in a way that I couldn't before. It also gave me opportunities to reconnect to my culture and explore or do things without having to deal with my parents commenting on what I was wearing or that I came home late. Although these kind of comments didn't hold me back, I realized I could do these things without ever having to think about or hear any of that.

Without realizing sometimes, we naturally filter ourselves in life, in any situation. So, if you're living with people who love you, but maybe don't quite accept or understand who you are, and you're having to filter yourself, that takes energy from you. Would you describe this time as a new beginning? It sounds as if COVID happened, and then a few years later you were with your partner in your lovely new home together. How did this new beginning feel for you?

It felt great in a lot of ways. When I was moving out, one of the things I said to my mum was that I couldn't live with never being able to eat the food that I loved, so I spent time with her learning some of my favourite recipes. That was a great way to feel reconnected to my culture. Every time I cook one of my favourite meals, it feels like home. It feels as if I'm part of something, I'm part of this culture, this community, even though that community will say I'm not; I'm part of it in my own way, in a way that I enjoy.

Everything's quite new. I get to have house parties and I invite all the people I've collected along the way and made part of my community. It's lovely to have the people I know connecting with the other people I know; it really feels as if I'm forming the community that I always wanted.

It's beautiful because you're creating the change that you wanted, and what you wanted to see but couldn't find. You've done that yourself and I think that's incredibly powerful and inspiring.

Yeah, and because my partner is not Asian, there's a part of me that wants to make sure that doesn't get lost. I feel like I am indulging in my culture in more ways than I did before; a lot of the stuff that became routine before has now become more important. It means a lot to be able to share that culture with someone, or to invite people over to celebrate Diwali, for example.

When we moved into our new house we had a party, and because we had it in October, it was my partner's birthday, Halloween, but it was also Diwali. We had this big combination party, and we decorated the whole kitchen in celebratory things for Diwali. We put up signs and decorative flowers. I cooked two big dishes, and I got a bunch of stuff from the local shop and served it all up for everyone. Everyone was eating samosas, pakoras and butter chicken, food that I'd made.

We all had sparklers outside, and that was a lovely way to reconnect to the community, and share my community, the community that I felt I'd lost, but with the people that I now have; it was a nice moment for me. I go out with my partner in traditional Indian dresswear and we go to the local temple together, and I'm connecting with my culture in a way that is important to me.

It's great that you've been able to capture that and then bring it into your friends' lives as well. That's just a wonderful thing. For you, does it feel as if you're bringing your whole self to

every situation: your sexuality, your gender, your culture? It must feel really fulfilling for you.

It does, especially when we've had moments where I've dressed up in my clothing with my partner, or I've had a party where I've served food and decorated the house, and explained the culture to the people we are with. I really feel I'm bringing my whole self to the people who are there for me, who care about me, and they reciprocate. They accept, see and love me for that, in a way that I never really had from people before. When I would take that whole self to any of my other communities, I felt rejected. Now I get to do that, and I'm embraced.

Do you feel that you've personally gained anything because of these experiences?

Trauma! Yeah, there has been trauma that I've gained because of everything, and I am constantly working on that. There are always things that I'm trying to deal with. I love my friends and my chosen family, but I've had so much trauma with friendships falling out that I'm still working out how to make sure I am interacting with them, not exhausting myself, and having reciprocal friendships. I'm working out how I deal with things, especially when difficult conversations come up. How do I have those conversations without anxiety and fear that they are going to reject me?

In a more positive sense, these experiences have given me a broader worldview. I think some straight people don't realize a lot of things because they're so wrapped up in the normality of it all, and they don't get that wider perspective. They find a partner in some form of institution, whether that be high school, university or the workplace, get together, get married, have kids, get a house, get a car. It's just a complete normative idea of what it means to live and to exist. They'll have friends who they've known for years, but who also don't share any of the same beliefs as them, which is baffling to me.

I know people who are best friends, who've been together for ages, they're both queer, and they've bought a house together. I couldn't imagine a straight person doing that. There are so many things such as the way we exist, the way that we move through the world, dress, act and talk, that I feel have opened my eyes to different ways of living, being, existing and interacting with the world. That's why I love the word queer so much as well; that it's queering this worldview, and it's so much more beyond sexuality. It's like, what does it mean to be Asian? What does it mean to enjoy this culture? What does it mean to be a man or a woman? What does it mean to be anything? And I think that it's given me a broader worldview in terms of who I am and my identity.

Do you think, with all the understanding that you have now of the losses you've encountered, and the way you've handled them, that it was unique to you as a queer person and maybe someone who wasn't queer wouldn't have the same experiences?
I guess so, but it's hard to quantify when you don't know what it means to exist outside it. How I move through the world is dictated by who I am. I really notice that a lot with class, more than anything else. My parents come from a very working-class background and they instilled in us a working-class mindset: work, save, constantly worry about money. I went to university and I've got a very well-paid job. I'm now surrounded by people who are maybe more middle-class and I realize that they have a completely different mindset.

When I look at that, I can see that a lot of the ways that I dealt with things in my life, and the ways that I navigated my life, have been dictated by who I am. So, if you extrapolate that, the ways that I dealt with things are because I'm queer, and because I'm a person of colour. The way I've navigated my life and the ways I've interacted with things and the path I've taken have been because of who I am.

Why do you think it's important, for individuals to speak about experiences of loss?

It makes it easier for other people to speak out. Loss can be something that's incredibly traumatic and can impact you in a variety of different ways. It can change who you are, the way you go through the world, your whole personality, and your life.

Openly talking about loss can remove the stigma of talking about mental health. Ultimately, losing things can cause trauma, which impacts mental health and your well-being; openly talking about it can be very cathartic as a personal experience, but it can also help remove the stigma for others.

Do you feel that with everything you've gone through, and the losses that you've dealt with, it's made you more resilient in life?

Yes and no. Yes, in that I know I can get through anything as I've hit rock bottom and I know what rock bottom feels like. I know that if I manage to survive that, I can survive anything else that life throws at me.

It has also made me more delicate and empathetic. It's brought out a lot of empathy, so when I see things that happen in the world, or when I go through things, I guess I am more moved by it, and more than I otherwise would have been because it brings me back to my own trauma and experiences.

Do you think as a queer person or person in the queer community that understanding and exploring identity and sexuality, and your experiences with living authentically, have enabled you to deal with challenges in life, particularly around losses as and when they arise? If so, why do you think this is?
I think so, because doing something like understanding your queer identity means a lot of introspection. It means a lot of looking inwards, understanding yourself and understanding your being. Having spent so long doing this kind of reflection, when things happen and when you see things, you dig a little bit deeper and delve in, trying to understand it because you're used to doing that as a person.

Is there any advice that you would give to anyone who is a person of colour, or bisexual, who is coming into the community or trying to find their place, based on your own experiences?
I would always say to never sacrifice yourself, no matter the consequences. There was a point in my life, when I was about 14 years old, where I felt I was at a crossroads. I could go one way and do all this stuff and then not have to deal with all the hardship, but that would make me depressed. If I went the other way, I would have to deal with a lot of the hardship and I would probably still be depressed, but at least I would get to enjoy who I am and be me, and ultimately that's the route I took.

It wasn't easy. There were many difficulties, homophobia, bigotry and being shunned and losing community, but ultimately at least I got to be me, rather than being someone I'm not, because that would have hurt a lot more. So never sacrifice who you are. Whether that means losing a community, or losing a space, I think that's more important. And the other thing I would say is that no space is ever without its problems – that's the unfortunate reality, you're always going to find problems within a community.

Ultimately, you must take what you can from it, and that means finding the places within that community that you can enjoy, finding the people you can enjoy, making and carving out a space for yourself where you can exist, you can be you, and trying to keep yourself safe from anything else outside that.

Do you believe in life after loss? And if you do, how long did it take you to feel that way?
I do, and it took me a long time to believe in that because for a long time, I probably should have mentioned this earlier in our conversation, I was very suicidal. I dealt with suicidal ideation for a very, very long time. I didn't believe there was a life worth living because I felt I was shunned from everything and there was nothing left for me, no community, no friends, no people. There was no way to exist as who I was. It's only in the last couple of years that I've understood that it does get better, because it really did.

It took me a long time to realize that; 2017 was rock bottom, and it was only in 2020 that I really felt I was moving out from that, and in the last two years where I really felt like I was looking forward to life in a way that I never really had before.

What people don't tell you is what it means to look forward to life. I'm now this age and I've got all these things I want to do. I feel I'm running out of time, and wondering how long I have left. For a long time, I felt if I die tomorrow, that's fine, who cares? And now, there's a life to be lived and enjoyed.

Ask Silva

As we can see from Vaneet's experiences, finding a community and a sense of belonging can be challenging. How important is it for queer people to find their people and chosen family, and what value can this add to their life?

It is now widely accepted among queer therapists that having a chosen family is paramount to the well-being of queer people, especially if the family of origin is not accepting. But even if the family of origin is good, a chosen family is still important because they are made up of people who really understand what it is like to be queer from the heart, not only the intellectual and political version of our lives.

Some people use the words 'chosen family' and 'community' interchangeably, but for others, there is a difference between the two. Some queer people experience the queer community as harsh and rejecting, whereas their chosen family made up of carefully selected queer people is their safe place.

One of the reasons that the queer community can be harsh is because we are an ostracized and traumatized community, so, in an attempt to survive, we avoid vulnerability and meaningful connection, even though it is what we deeply need the most. Within a chosen family, queer people can truly thrive and access queer joy, rather than merely existing and surviving.

CHAPTER 7

Loss of Opportunity

Luciana Cousin

Age: 61
Pronouns: She/Her
Sexual orientation/identity: Lesbian
Occupation: Director/Entrepreneur
Home town: Brighton, UK

Luciana's life journey unfolded across continents, growing up in Malta, moving to the USA, then finally 15 years ago, moving to Brighton where she started to feel as if she fitted in and belonged. As the co-founder of Across Rainbows Community Interest Company with her son Nick and owner of Arcobaleno, an LGBTQ+ café/bar in Brighton, she transformed her personal struggle into a mission. Through Across Rainbows, Arcobaleno and the street safety initiative Back Off. Back Up, Luciana champions transformative dialogues. Her work exemplifies a dedication to creating a world where conversations pave the way for a more inclusive and understanding society.

In this interview, I speak with Luciana about her experience of a loss of opportunity within her life, as a result of her gender, Catholic upbringing and sexuality. Please be aware that this interview makes references to divorce, homelessness, mental health difficulties and sex.

How do you manage an ending or a loss when it's presented to you?
I tend to get a bit practical. Someone close to me is going through a situation where her husband is dying and he's been given his last days. I'm just in organization mode, telling her what she needs to do. I hear myself and I think, shut up, she doesn't need to know that. I think it's just needing to have control.

Is it a way of avoiding the pain of a loss? Practical first, and then the emotion comes later?
Yeah, because I could also go in the other direction, where I'd be so emotional that I couldn't do anything. I feel especially with endings, you don't know what's going to happen next. Every ending has a beginning. This is totally unrelated, but now I'm fixated on death, because I really don't know what's going to happen; no one can tell me what happens next. We all know it's going to happen, but no one really knows, so that does make me feel a bit uncomfortable.

Can you share with me your personal experience of loss?
Growing up in Malta, a very small island, very Catholic, your

gender dictated your role in life. It wasn't just from the moment you left the hospital, it was throughout your life: where you went to school, the subjects you studied, a preordained plan for you based on your gender. Now, it's probably quite a bit different. So there was never an opportunity to question, because it was like being placed on a factory belt; girl, you go to this school, you study these subjects. It's not worth you going to university because you're going to get married. Then you get married and have the children.

I didn't know better, so I followed, and you didn't question it. As a child, it's the norm because everybody else is doing it, but I always had a feeling of being different. One of the things that always bothered me was getting married.

I wanted to be a lawyer, but when it came to going into further education and training, my father said it was better to invest the money in my brother, because, after all, I was going to get married. That was the second time being a girl didn't work for me. The first time was when I was seven and I wanted to be an altar boy. I kept asking, why can't I be an altar boy? It was only that I liked the costume they wore; meanwhile they were begging my brother, who couldn't give two shits about doing it. They said that girls couldn't be altar boys, so I think that's when I fell out with the church, at the age of seven.

The school I went to was a convent where they recruit you to become a nun, so from every class they expect to have three or four girls at age 14 say they want to be a nun. Every single person just touches on things, and considers their options, but then I started thinking, if you're a nun, you can't do that, so the nunnery was out. The other option was marriage. You get the well-meaning relative asking if you have a boyfriend, followed by, 'What's wrong? You're so pretty. You should have so many boyfriends.' I didn't, but nothing was clicking yet, I just thought I didn't like boys.

I then had a major friendship with a girl. I was totally immersed in that friendship. That was the very first time I think something sort of clicked, and when she got a boyfriend, I was heartbroken.

We then fast forward, and I met this other person. I always liked stories and theirs, which was 30 years ago now, was that they didn't fit in and thought they were different. We didn't have words for what these differences were at that time. They were a totally unsuitable person, they weren't Maltese, they were going to emigrate to America, and I was like, yeah, I'm there.

Obviously by this time I had figured out who I was, but I knew that I couldn't act on it because of the family. I know it sounds weird now, but in those days, they were putting gay people in my country in jail.

How old were you when your friend got the boyfriend, and you were heartbroken, and when you started to understand who you were and more about your sexuality?

I was 16 when my friend met her boyfriend. I got married when I was 17; that heartbreak, looking back, was the trigger that started everything. I went to America, had the children, but I've never been in another marriage, so I can't tell you if it was right or wrong, I don't know. We just lived; we were two people in survival mode, because we were both doing something we didn't want to do.

When the kids came I made a conscious decision to be the best mother I could be. We were in America and, of course, I had access to different things, and so we lived very separate lives, but outwardly, we were like the perfect family.

It sounds as if it was a marriage of convenience because you both were looking for something that you couldn't have, so maybe you found safety in each other?
Marriage of convenience yes, but not safety, because what I experienced was incredible loneliness. Even though I was able to pursue relationships – let's call them extreme friendships – it was always a case of being on a stage and pretending. Society expected me to be this mother and supportive wife, but my ex-partner did not want any of that, so the pieces never did fit together.

Eventually I left, and by that time I was wiped out financially. At one point, I lived in a car for three days with my son, because I had nowhere to go.

From what I am hearing, there's the loss of opportunity from being a girl in a Catholic country, your role, expectations and what you should and shouldn't do because of your gender. You met someone and found a kinship because you were both going through something that is so difficult to deal with, and it seems this was a way of survival and getting through. Then you had this feeling of isolation, because you couldn't authentically be you. How would you describe your feelings during that time?
It was incredible loneliness, and I couldn't really understand myself. We lived in a beautiful house. The children were happy, everybody had what they wanted. I used to think, why am I so miserable? I kept thinking it was me, I was just ungrateful. Eventually, I went to therapy and the therapist said, if I had had

the supportive family, I'd have become a lawyer, and life would have been completely different; it was the first time someone verbalized that, and the first time I thought, actually, yeah, I could have had a completely different life.

Would you have been able to be open about your sexuality at that time? Even if you'd become a lawyer, or do you think that wouldn't have mattered so much, because you'd have had other opportunities?

I think I'd have had other opportunities, and because it would have been about the career, as it was for most of us in the 1980s and 90s, there wouldn't have been that pressure to get married and have children. The idea was that your career became your life. Something I am very passionate about, and something we focus on at Across Rainbows, is identity. I'm obsessed by it because I think knowing who you are is central to your existence, and to the choices you make. Back then, I wasn't even able to make choices.

I hope this is not too personal, but during that time, did you have an opportunity to form other relationships and explore your sexuality?

Yes, and when you want something, the universe makes it happen! We lived in a house, and there were two women who lived nearby. This was remote, and in the countryside, so I guess they were trying to get away from the world. That was a very interesting time because my ex-partner used to travel for business a lot. So, ta da!

I love that! It sounds as if you found an understanding of the

situation you were in. Would it be right to say that you didn't have much support around you at that time?

My ex-partner changed their name, so I couldn't get a divorce, and at the time I could not contact them. With my family being Catholic, divorce is one of the top five reasons for being disowned, so I was quite alone.

So, you'd had therapy, understood the loss in terms of your opportunities, and decided your marriage couldn't continue. Is it bittersweet in a way, because on one hand, there was a lost opportunity, but also if the opportunity had been there, you wouldn't have had your children and now your grandchildren. So, when you look back at that loss, although it's difficult, do you think that there was a positive that came out of it as well?

Yes, like I said, the children became my whole life. I mean, I was a helicopter mum before helicopters were invented, but eventually children have their own lives. They have known for a long time, so I don't feel they were lied to. I do feel that I wasn't able to be myself with them sometimes. So, even though I could never act on a stage, I could act these roles I created, and you end up getting very good at it.

How would you describe the time that you thought you could do this by yourself and move forward?

The children were in my life and there was a reason. My youngest son is very sensitive – he was the baby who picked up on everything. If I looked sad, his whole day would be ruined. So, I'd have to put on a sort of show, and in those days of us sleeping in the car, I created an adventure that it was my choice to show him what it was like to do this.

I called my accountant and I said, I didn't know where to go. He knew I worked in marketing, and told me he had a client in Derby who owned a hotel, and said I could work and live there during the week. We were in the UK, but I didn't even know where Derby was. So, I started doing that; my son was in boarding school at this time, that's why it was easy to manage. I used to pick him up on a Saturday and we'd go to my aunt in Essex, and then back again. There was a lot of driving!

I went to London one day and somebody handed me a leaflet for a networking event, and I decided to go. There were maybe 80 people there, and across the room there was this one person and we just locked eyes and gravitated to each other. She was a coach, we started talking and made plans to meet; she was very helpful in many ways. Over the next two or three years, we started a company together and I got on my feet that way.

I was still living two lives. I'd have the lesbian me and the straight me, and I was convinced clients would leave if they knew. Then, one day, my son started questioning his sexuality and I decided that this time it would be different, but it needed to start with me. So, I just woke up in the morning, called everyone I knew and said, okay, this is the situation, this is who I am, you now make the decision, if you want to be in my life or not. It was the biggest relief because I knew if I didn't put my head above the parapet, there was no way I was going to be able to help my son get through this. And what example was I setting?

What did that feel like, to get that out of your body and finally be able to express who you were?
The days leading up to it were terrifying. But when I did it, I mean, I'm not a big person, but I did feel a lot taller! There

was a lot of freedom. People said, oh my goodness, why would you want to do this now? You have a good life, why would you want to mess it up? I also realized that coming out wasn't for other people, it was for me. I made the decision I was not going to get into a long-term relationship because by being in one in my twenties and thirties, I had missed two decades! I had a really good time!

Was it like reclaiming your youth because you'd missed out on the opportunity?
Yes, it was.

I've been thinking about loss of youth quite a lot recently, and what this means to me personally. I've got friends who are younger than me, and the way they see the world, the way they see queerness, being gay, however you want to phrase it, is completely different from my experience of being their age. I'm reflecting on that, and grieving for the youth that I didn't have.
Yeah, I totally agree. I think it's because of the set-in-stone patriarchal society. I was robbed, and I do grieve that a lot. I try not to have regrets because it all ended up well, but it bothers me that I didn't have choices and wasn't in control of what happened next. It wasn't even an expectation, it was a dictation.

When my father passed away, he had been sick for a few months and I was going back to Malta and I was going to tell him, because I thought before he dies, he should know. But I never got a chance. Sometimes I think maybe it's better that way, I didn't spoil any illusions for him. But on the other hand, we can tell the stories we want to hear, right? Maybe he would have been okay with it.

I'm really interested to talk about the next phase of your life because the phrase lemons into lemonade springs to mind, when I think about what you are achieving now. It's incredible! Can you talk to me about Across Rainbows, the charity you founded, which is focused on understanding and exploring identity, and how that was born? We should also talk about Arcobaleno, your venue in the heart of Kemptown, Brighton, UK, and of course Back Off. Back Up, the app you created to identify queer friendly venues and support community safety. With Across Rainbows, I had written the business plan almost 15 years ago, and two, three times a week I'd work on it. It was always with the hope it was going somewhere. I knew what Arcobaleno would look like. I must credit my partner, because she believes in me as me, and that kind of support changed everything for me. I've never had somebody believe in me or tell me I could do something, and I did not trust what she was saying for years.

Across Rainbows was born from the need to belong somewhere, to be seen, to be heard, because I felt very much that I was invisible for most of my life. I was either someone's daughter, someone's mother, someone's wife, but never me. My son was getting really bullied at school and there were two other kids getting bullied too; I was a business consultant at the time, had no idea how to help him, but I decided to look at the situation like a business problem. We sat at the kitchen table and did just that; it was about building confidence and having self-worth, and that's how it all started.

I moved to London and then we started running workshops. During COVID, a few of our friends were really struggling, so we started bubbles, which is where we'd sit in the garden because you were allowed to do that, and just talk about the things we were dealing with. Throughout this time, I'd go and see properties; I never liked anything and didn't even have the money, but I'd go just in case. One day, the agent called me and said there was a property that had just come up and was just what I was looking for. This was three years after I gave them the brief. The property was a disaster, but it was exactly what I wanted, and so then things started coming together. Arcobaleno is the physical representation of Across Rainbows.

During COVID, another friend of ours was out with his boyfriend and they got beaten up, but they had nowhere to go because all the venues kept saying, we can't leave our spot, you can't come in, so no one supported them. That's how Back Off. Back Up started; it was a very simple idea, but it's grown into quite an initiative, and there is so much that we can do with it.

Honestly, it makes me a bit emotional when I hear you telling the story. For me, when you have difficulties and then you create something so wonderful, it's inspiring for others. You've gone from a lack of choice in your life to now being in a situation where you have multiple businesses which help people to live their best lives, feel safe, meet people who mirror who they are, and you've created that. How does that feel?

Andrew, I think this is the moment of truth for your book. It takes me a lot to let go of the past. Sometimes I get angry, and I think, this could have been done 20 years ago. Sometimes I'm sad that I didn't have the capacity to put my foot down and say, no, I'm not doing this, because there is so much to do, and so little time. I feel those 20 years that I spent in the darkness took away from what could have been.

When you said you were writing this book, I said, maybe I need to grieve to let go, instead of being angry about it. There are the five stages of grief, but I'm always in the angry or sad mode. I tell myself, at least you're doing it now, but how did it help anyone for me to go through that, such a dislocated past? You might say that I had the children from it, but there may have been another way to have those children.

Your choice was taken from you, wasn't it? You're not wrong for feeling those things. I guess another way to look at it is that you have a son who is living his best life, has so many dreams, and is making such an impact on our community, because he has a mother who has told him that anything is possible. That makes my heart so warm.

Thank you. Maybe I should grieve rather than just take everything on board and say, well, that's happened now. When I started rebuilding my life, I was below zero. So, it wasn't even a level playing field. I also had no clue what the hell I was doing, but I think for the longest time, I just kept looking forward, not worrying about anything else.

Looking back, what would you do differently?

When I was growing up, there were gay people, gay kids, very closeted, but they found a way, and they were in the actor's group at school. I was so terrified of doing the wrong thing. I wanted so desperately to be a lawyer, so I went to America, where there are possibilities with education, but I didn't pursue it because I wanted to be the good person. So, I think maybe I'd be less good and not do exactly what people expected of me.

I'm interested to know how it feels being in the position you are now with everything you've known and learned. We've talked about Arcobaleno, Across Rainbows, Back Off. Back Up.

How does it feel for you as a person of the community to be putting something back out there and turning a very difficult situation into something so amazing? I know you're working hard, but how does that feel to you personally?

I'm humbled. I'm constantly amazed by people's stories, and what they go through. I'm blessed that I was able to create a space. It comes with a lot of responsibility to make sure that everyone is being seen, and so when it does happen, I feel humbled by that. I get teary-eyed because somebody will do something or say something. One person literally came to Arcobaleno every afternoon, didn't say a word, and recently just started talking. We have these little ten-second conversations, but they're getting longer. It's those little things. My biggest challenge is aligning profit and passion because the two do not go. You can't always be profitable and be doing a purposeful thing. So, it takes time.

This is not a financial thing for us, and I'm more than okay with that. If we keep the lights on, roof on, create these performances and events, and a place where people can go and everything is reasonably priced, I'm okay with that. But yes, it's just humbling.

Do you think, with all the understanding you have now, that the way you handled your loss was unique to you as a queer person, and do you think that someone who doesn't identify within our community would have had the same experience?

I think it was the resilience, let's call it that, of waking up every morning and knowing I needed to get through the day. A lot of that was down to having a young child because they needed to eat, they needed a roof over their head. So, I was almost secondary. The difference was when I could, I put myself in situations where I could choose. So, I chose to have a business, I chose to work with women-owned businesses, I decided I was done living a double life. Some people cut their hair, some people change their clothes, it's almost as if there's a rebirth. I'm not saying that you need to learn how to be this lesbian, but I think for me, it gave me a lot more confidence. It gave me a lot more identity. It helped me to keep moving forward more positively, rather than always having that void.

Do you think understanding and exploring your identity, sexuality and living more authentically have supported you with becoming more resilient in life?

I think the resilience happened before, because you end up being so in yourself, and you only have yourself to rely on, that the resilience grows, and you learn how to do things alone, and be alone. If you want something, there's no one you can depend on, you've got to go and get it yourself. I think the pre-coming out period does build up a lot of resilience and courage as well, and there's a lot of courage in the community. I'm proud to be me; it's very difficult to explain this, but it's not about the achievements or the hard work, it's just about being me, and it gives me so much pleasure when people see me, and they want to talk to me. It's not because they want something, but because they want to talk to me because this is who I am. With my son Nick, we have such a great relationship because he gets it, he sees me.

Do you think that's because for so long, you had to hide, so to be seen is a validation?

Yes, and our tagline for Across Rainbows is that every single person is seen and heard, because I think when people are seen and heard, it does something for their confidence and self-worth.

What advice would you give to anyone coming to terms with who they are or dealing with a loss where they're having to move forward with their lives?
It's about being kind to yourself. I've had to learn that as well. Sometimes, I didn't even like what I was doing to myself, I was so harsh, and I'd never do it to anyone else. It's being kind to yourself, knowing yourself and what you want and need in your life.

Finally, do you believe in life after loss, and how long did it take you to feel that way?
I do believe in life after loss. I think the life after the loss was almost parallel to life going on. The grieving never really stops, it just changes, but life does move forward.

Since this interview took place, Luciana and her family had to make the heartbreaking decision of closing Arcobaleno. Arcobaleno was such a beautiful and unique venue in Kemptown, Brighton. My friend and I were discussing this recently, and put simply, the venue had heart. I personally have so many fond memories of time spent at Arcobaleno and can only imagine how difficult the decision to close was for Luciana and her family. I guess this is a reminder that Queer venues are sacred, and if we don't use them, our opportunities as a community to go to venues that are safe spaces and enable us the freedom to unapologetically be ourselves will reduce. Reader, where you can, please support queer spaces; they are so important.

Ask Silva

As Luciana experienced, the opportunity to live authentically and openly is not always possible for queer people. How can filtering one's identity affect their mental health and what impact can this have on day-to-day life and taking space in the world as a queer person?

In studies, there is a clear correlation between poor mental health and repressing one's authentic sexuality and gender identity. Some queer people who struggle to accept their sexuality and gender identity will tend to feel more depressed, and some will have suicidal ideations. However, it is also important to think about the queer people who live in dangerous places, such as countries that criminalize same-sex relationships, or people who live in violent homophobic and transphobic households around the world, where coming out is not safe.

Repressing one's sexuality or gender identity to avoid serious violence and potential death will obviously need to take priority over coming out. So, it is important to think about the context too. For most people living in the UK and not being in such violent households, the struggle to accept one's sexuality and gender identity may be to do with internalized homophobia (a core belief learned and conditioned from childhood that being gay is bad), which can be detrimental to well-being. Learning to accept one's sexuality and gender identity can be a long process, usually better facilitated with queer-affirming therapy. Indeed, taking space in the world as a queer person is a courageous and defiant act!

CHAPTER 8

Loss of Religious Community

Mendez

Age: 42
Pronouns: They/Them
Sexual orientation/identity: Queer/Non-binary
Occupation: Writer
Home town: Born in Dudley, reside in Margate, UK

Mendez is a novelist, screenwriter and critic. Their debut novel, Rainbow Milk, *was published in 2020 and shortlisted for the Gordon Burn, Polari and Jhalak prizes.*

In this interview, I speak with Mendez about their experience of a loss of religious community, due to their sexuality and identity. Please be aware that this interview makes references to death, homophobia, rejection, religion and sex.

How do you tend to manage endings or a loss when they're presented to you?

The first big loss I experienced was my relationship with my mother, and while our relationship broke down or was in the process of becoming irreparable, we still lived together for over ten years. In that kind of situation, you just have to manage as best you can. Another loss I sustained was that of my religious community, the doctrine, and having to overcome that. I threw myself into being and doing exactly the opposite of everything that I had ever been raised to be or believe. This was made somewhat easier by the fact that queer life and experience and queer experimentation are completely anathema to my religious community.

How old were you when you encountered this loss?

I was 17 years old when I left the Jehovah's Witness community. I still stuck around for a little while, scratching at the back door, trying to get back in like an abandoned cat. But it was maybe another two years, so probably I was 19 or 20 years old, when I realized that there was no going back.

The decisions that I would make going forward would be regardless of whether my parents, for example, would forgive me or accept my truth. And so that was a completely all-encompassing loss really, because not only was I losing my religion, but I was also losing the belief of living forever on a paradise Earth (the belief of the community) and that everyone who's not a Jehovah's Witness will die at Armageddon.

I was raised to believe that no one outside the organization was to be trusted or associated with, and that they were all doomed. I was taught that we were the only ones who would inherit the Earth. So, when you've got that as a long-term belief, together with the idea of living forever and that you'll never die – losing that is a huge thing. You lose your entire community who are so brainwashed that they think that you're completely stupid for choosing to live some other truth, as you put it, rather than live *the* truth, which is how the Witnesses refer to their beliefs. So, you lose your image, your reputation, your family, your extended family, your spiritual family, your dignity and your direction.

As human beings, generally speaking, we hold the idea that we'll probably live to 70 or 80 years old and then die, but as a Jehovah's Witness, you hold an eternal purpose; I don't think you can really overestimate the loss of that super purpose and what it does to you as a young person.

Do you remember the exact point in time when you realized that you had to choose living outside your community, and what was the catalyst for you making that decision?
It was around the summer of 2002 or 2003. They were the first two summers I was living away from my family. I was living in Kent and my family were in the Midlands; I was being introduced to different literature, different music, different films, a different way of looking at the world. In fact, it sounds quite trivial, but there was a magazine – I think it was an early issue of *AnOther* – featuring an article entitled 'In praise of beautiful men', which I read; it hadn't occurred to me before that I, someone who was raised as a boy, could appreciate beauty in men. Of course I did, inwardly, but it wasn't until I read that article that I realized that I could do that outwardly as well, and that it was a possibility for me. Up until then I'd had girlfriends and

tried my best to fit into a very heterosexual environment, but it was through reading this article that I admitted that men were attractive to me. This led me to come out initially as bisexual, but it was with the idea that, as I alluded to earlier, if I had to spend the rest of my life avoiding my family, or if I was never able to speak to my family again because of this, then so be it, because they were going to be very much centred on their beliefs. I was 21 years old when I made that decision.

That's quite a decision to make. Thank you for sharing that. Was there something at that point in time that gave you the courage to outwardly make the decision, affirm who you were and walk away?
Writing, predominantly. When I was 20, I started writing properly. Having that inner voice and having the ability to self-reflect on paper, having the language, having the presence of mind to do that, armed me to overcome what I was reacting against.

My early writing from that era was very angry, cathartic outpourings, very fire-and-brimstone, measuring the tyranny of my previous beliefs with my present reality at that time. I was connecting the decisions and I basically saw myself hurtling into this sort of hellfire situation. I used writing almost as a form of therapy and to check in with myself to see what my brain was doing at that point; it gave me the power to continue along that road. And of course, reading. That was the period in which I had started to read James Baldwin, Toni Morrison, Angela Carter, writers whose experience as queer people, as black people, as women, pointed the way forward for me to auto-theorize almost, and use myself and my own experiences at the centre of a discussion about survival and what it means to be part of a family, what it means to have belief and faith, and what it means to take a step back from the world in which you're raised because there's nothing you can do about that while you're a child.

It's during early adulthood, during your young years away from family for the first time, that you have the space to be able to do that, not under their supervision or tyranny.

Do you remember the feelings you experienced around that time, after you had made that difficult decision?
I had no choice but to continue along a different path. I was living with a load of art students, and these were the first free-thinking people I'd ever met. We had the music of the early 2000s. It was a very interesting time.

I came out and made all of these decisions in 2003. That was the year that Section 28 was repealed. I didn't know anything about Section 28 at the time. I just lived through it, like a lot of other queer people. Section 28 was very insidious; it got sworn into law when I was six years old, and I wouldn't have known a thing, but I certainly lived through it. It was repealed when I was 21 years old, in the year that I came out. I saw myself casting myself into the abyss, but need there be an abyss? These are the sorts of questions that I was starting to ask myself; I was reading, being exposed to new music and films, hanging out with these free-thinking people, realizing that my sexuality wasn't something necessarily punishable by death.

When you grow up with Section 28 and with the AIDS crisis, that's what you think of yourself, and it takes a long time to de-indoctrinate yourself of that, deconstruct that kind of self-defeating behaviour. When I was living through this, I think my feelings were very optimistic, and I felt a sense of freedom, even though looking back now, I probably wasn't that free yet. I'm still on a journey towards feeling truly free, but it was certainly a start and very positive. I had a lot of curiosity about the world that I'd been told to turn my back on and told was about to end; it's still here! There was almost a childlike curiosity about the world and my place in it.

You've talked about a sense of freedom, but obviously we're talking about the loss of your religious community. While you felt a loss, was there a relief as well, that you could choose a different path and that you didn't have to comply with what you'd been taught over the years?

I did feel a sense of relief. I mean, it's both really. I felt relieved to not be under their surveillance any more, but these are people you've grown up with all your life. These are people you call aunty and uncle even though they're not blood relatives. Part of the reason behind their practice of disfellowshipping, rendering you uncommunicable, is to shame you, make you feel guilty and lost. That loss should feel so painful that you repent of everything that you've done immediately and wait to be accepted back. I was disfellowshipped when I was 17. It was nothing to do with me being gay; that part of *Rainbow Milk* is completely fictionalized. I was reinstated at 19 years old, and then actually thought, you know what, this isn't for me. There was a four-year gap between being disfellowshipped and finally coming out.

I guess by that time I started to build a new community around myself, which aided my decision to live by my own truth. I think if I'd stayed in the Midlands, it wouldn't have been as easy to live the life that I wanted to live.

It sounds as if you had a good support network around you as well during that time of transition from old life to new life. Were you celebrated for being you, and did you feel a sense of acceptance and liberation in that respect?

Up to a point. I initially came out as bisexual, so there was a reticence on my part, as I still wasn't comfortable with the term gay. I was outed actually once or twice by these so-called protective people, and I guess they would say they were joking or playing, but I probably came from a much less liberal place than they were used to, so it was very hurtful to me to be outed before I was ready.

It was really when I moved to London in 2004 that I started to lean into a gay identity properly and to surround myself with more affirming people. On my first day in London, 6 July 2004, I was living with this guy who I was introduced to by a mutual friend of ours in Birmingham. We were chatting at his dining table, and he was rolling a huge spliff, and then we went into the front room, and he put on John Waters' *Female Trouble*. It was the first time I'd seen anything like this, like any kind of queer, subversive, camp cinema. As I grew up, if I was allowed any access to queer people at all through my childhood, it was people like Lily Savage, comedians like Dame Edna Everage, or people who, for one reason or another, hoodwinked us to believe they were straight, and then once their sexuality or the truth of their sexuality was known, it was almost as if they were buried in my household.

Watching John Waters' *Female Trouble*, my mind was

absolutely blown, and that started me on a new journey towards queerness. I look at gay as being a sexual identity; there's a culture around it, of course, but I think queerness is that and more. Queerness includes gender, identity, who you are, your place in the world, your politics, all of those things; it's much more than a sexual orientation. As Section 28 was repealed, all the noise was around sexual orientation and the push towards equal marriage rights, so for years, gender identity and expression weren't really on the agenda for me.

But it was an exciting journey, and out of loss always comes creation. I've always had that idea that sometimes you have to destroy something in order for the ground to nourish new life, new creativity, and so that's what I did in my own life.

So, from 2004 onwards, you're rebuilding life, accepting who you are, but also processing your loss. What were those years like for you, and how did you process everything you'd been through to live authentically day to day?
I was in London studying acting at a school that didn't offer a degree but a certificate, so I couldn't get a student loan for it. I needed to find quite a lot of money to be able to pay my fees and pay my rent, so, it was suggested to me by this person I was living with that I do sex work.

I'd been out by this point for a year. I was very sexually active, very open-minded in terms of who I slept with, so it didn't feel like a huge step out of the ordinary for me. It was a way to deal with the loss and also to process or further the de-indoctrination. You know, if the Jehovah's Witnesses find homosexuality anathema, then I shall demolish the wall by becoming a sex worker, a queer sex worker. There was a little bit of bravado, a little bit of self-destructiveness that had crept in there, but I was 22 years old and I thought I was invincible. I wouldn't do it now, but I was stupid enough back then to use that as a way of healing.

Do you think it helped to heal you?
In some ways it really did take me as far away from the doctrine as possible, but I think it was too much too soon. I was living in a new city; I didn't know anybody when I first moved to London. I had this person who I was living with at the beginning, but that was only a temporary arrangement and I moved into a gay house-share in Tottenham. I got on perfectly well with everyone in the house, but I still hadn't known any of them for more than a couple of months, so there wasn't really anybody I could rely on for support at this time, especially when I was putting myself in danger and making myself quite vulnerable.

It was both a lesson in survival, but also a warning against putting myself in certain positions for the sake of some kind of heroism. Nobody stands to benefit if you die or if you go too far into trying to prove something. It was a difficult and a messy time; I sort of look back on it with some fondness though because I was part of a queer community in a very peripheral way, admittedly. I was, however, living a queer life and questioning everything that I'd been brought up to believe. I was throwing myself into situations I'd never been in before and had to navigate.

I was meeting new people, who were introducing me to new literatures and new philosophies, who helped me to figure out my own identity. You know, that's when I first read Alan Hollinghurst. It's when I first read Huysmans and Baudelaire, all of these 19th and 20th century icons of subversive thought. I'm sure I didn't know how to handle it at the time, but once you plant those seeds, then it's only a matter of time until they take root.

I was writing at this point. The acting school thing didn't work for me, and I quit after a few months, but by this time I was really writing. So much of my experience at that time, so much of my writing, ended up as *Rainbow Milk*. Writing has really been my saviour in many ways.

We talk about the concept of chosen family; did you have an opportunity during those years to find one within the queer community that helped you to heal and look at the concept of a family in a different way?
It wasn't until maybe 2009 or 2010 that I started to build a chosen family around myself, a queer chosen family. I made friends outside what I would consider my chosen family, and there are people I know who I met in 2002 onwards, and they're still in my life and that's a wonderful thing.

In terms of a queer chosen family, it was 2009/2010, East London, and the bar scene there. I was going out four or five times a week, and that's where I met the community that I'm still part of in many ways. A lot of people moved away, and I moved to Margate but we're all still friends. It was about music and dancing. Once you were on the dance floor, the DJ was dropping whatever song, you were just very aware of the environment and of each other, and you didn't really care about anything because you'd left all of that at the door. So, it just became about that shared experience of love, and building those memories together; it was all about dressing up to be part of that, and to impress each other and exist within everyone's memories.

There have been moments where my reflex to reject, pull at everything and burn it down still applied here, but this community, this chosen family, without me even asking for it, have always offered that forgiveness in some way, because I think we're all part of that. We all have these destructive behaviours in common, I guess, because of us being queer people and having gone through what we've been through in order to be who we are and to live the truth. We understand that about each other. So, there is an unconditional love within the queer community as I know it.

Can you describe what life was like, as it was starting to move in a direction where you felt more settled and comfortable within yourself and the world around you?
I don't know, it's one of those questions where I think maybe I haven't yet settled.

As queer people, we're always, evolving, we're never settling, we're never still. I came out as non-binary last year and dropped my Christian names. So, even in my early forties, I don't think I'm there yet. I don't think I've completely overcome the loss I had to deal with, and that's fine. You know, I'm happy enough and I'm able to look after myself, but there's still a lot that's unresolved. There's still a lot that is yet to be fixed and is maybe unfixable.

Maybe I'm in a permanent state of flux, of perpetual flux, and that's fine. I have wonderful people in my life who are always holding me up, but I've just lost one of them, very sadly. As supportive as he was for me, I'm now part of that support group for his friends and even his mother. I've learned that through the love and the handholding that's been extended to me, and that I've relied on over the years. I don't think I've ever been in that place where I can say, I've overcome that now, because I'm still being affected on a daily basis by what I went through as a young person.

I really like what you said there, because we all think that we have to have everything solved or figured out in life to be happy, and I guess as hard as it can be at times, there is a beauty in the not knowing.

I think so. Of course, I've learned some lessons and I hope I don't make the same mistakes constantly. I mean, I do some of them actually, but I'm a product of art. You lose your parents' approval, you lose their backing, you lose their care; a child with little, if any, life experience relies on something very primal in order to survive that, and you build layers on top of that. You're constantly growing through this scar tissue, which is obviously not a good thing. So, I'm proud that I have survived up to this point and continue to survive, but I'm not a perfectly formed human being, and I will continue to fail and to make mistakes.

I also have an incredibly strong survival instinct and sense of destiny. Somehow, that's the reason why I'm still here and why I continue to enjoy life, create and make friends. In some ways I would rather be this well-adjusted, perfect person who is settled and has different problems, but I guess my nexus of problems and ways of dealing with things make me a unique person and writer. So, I'm thankful.

Do you think, with all the understanding you have now, that

your loss and the way you handled your loss were unique to you as a queer person, and that someone who isn't queer wouldn't necessarily have the same experience?

I think it made me brave enough to examine ways to deconstruct my previous mindset that a heterosexual, cisgender person wouldn't think of.

I think that's all really. This was a time before social media. People find it much easier now to assemble communities around themselves and find people with similar experiences. We had to wait for a magazine article or a documentary on Channel 4 or something like that. I think young queer people now have many more options than people our age; we had to go out looking for community, to find examples of other people going through the same or similar things. I had to be creative, I had to find my own ways of dealing with things; I'm not the sort of person who dwells and looks at all my options and lists pros and cons and then decides. I'm a very reactive person. I do what needs to be done on that day, for better or worse.

I don't feel I've had the luxury of sensible decision-making; that's largely how I've been raised by my parents. They were similar; they earned so little money that it was just like, okay, what can we do? What do we do? And if you've got like a little bit of extra one month, you're not going to save it, you're going to spend it because the six family members all need things. So, I've been raised with that sort of mindset, of feast or famine, and I guess I've applied that through every decision I've made. It would take some real sort of change in my life to break that.

Do you feel that as a queer person, understanding and exploring your identity, your sexuality and your experience of living

authentically has enabled you to deal with the challenges in life, in particular surrounding loss, and has it made you more resilient generally?

Yes and no. No, in a sense that it's always going to be difficult to not have the full support or to feel like you fully belong to your birth family, to your origin family. When things happen in the family, you can feel this sense of guilt for having extricated yourself from them. When they close ranks around a particular event, you can find yourself on the outside trying to reintegrate yourself. That can be really painful.

Times and people change. The family that I thought that I was escaping from – and I'm not talking about my parents, I'm talking about my extended family who aren't Jehovah's Witnesses – I left behind and then came back 10–15 years later to find them asking, 'When are we going to meet your boyfriend? What's your love life like?' I thought, who are these people who are all of a sudden accepting of my sexuality?

That can bring you down a little bit because you're gaslit into thinking that what you did, and the decisions that you made, were unnecessary. You could have had a chosen family and your origin family with you the whole time. It's hard to say whether me pursuing a queer identity has made me more resilient to loss. I don't know; it's something I'd have to think more about.

How important do you think it is for people to open up and share their experiences of loss?

We're so used to bottling things up and not moaning, not complaining. I think that kind of mentality needs to be disposed of, because we all come from trauma in some way. The more we share, the more we can begin to heal, both individually and as a community.

Of everything you've experienced so far, what do you think has been the most valuable lesson that you've learned through your personal journey?

To share your friends, to make sure your friends all know each other. As I've alluded to, I've recently lost a very close friend and it was a completely unexpected death. This was a queer person, and all of his friends were scattered around everywhere, but none of them knew each other. So, picking up the pieces, now that he's gone, we're having to seek each other out somehow and get to know each other after losing him. I wouldn't want that to happen to me. I'm very similar to him in terms of having friends from different eras and different aspects of my life, none of whom know each other. Because I didn't celebrate birthdays or Christmas as a child, I've never been used to hosting parties where everyone comes to celebrate me. Even when my book came out, I didn't have the opportunity to have a big book launch and invite everyone, because of the COVID pandemic.

So, it's a conscious decision that I have to make now going forward, to ensure that the people in my life all know each other, and to really treat it as a family rather than, 'I met this person then and I met that person there, so they can't know each other because they wouldn't get it.' I'll let them make that decision for themselves.

I want to make a real effort to celebrate myself and to allow other people to celebrate me and to be there for me. If I don't do that, I shall continue this sort of self-perpetuating idea that

I'm not worthy of being celebrated and being loved, and that is something that queer people tend to do. We all suffer in some way from this guilt complex, because of the persecution that we've faced. It's up to us in some way to demolish that.

Do you believe in life after loss? And if you do, how long did it take you to feel that way?
Yes, I do believe in life after loss. There's just so much to live for. We might think that the world is in a really bad place, and it is, but there's also a lot of love in the world, a lot of changeable minds whose views are based on a lack of first-hand experience. There's a lot to live for.

One way to process loss is to take on the best qualities of that thing that you've lost, or at least try to, and try to live your life augmented and decorated by those qualities. I definitely think that about my friend who I've just lost. What was it that I loved about him and what can I do to keep those qualities?

He was an extremely intellectually curious person and I know myself to be an extremely intellectually lazy person. So, that's one way in which I can ensure that the qualities he brought to the world haven't gone to waste, and that's one way to live after loss, I guess.

I think the people we lose never really leave us because when they're special enough, they leave a mark on our lives and our hearts. That's what I think when I've lost people in my life. Certain things will remind me of them: expressions, smells or places. It's an imprint on life. So, if you have all of that, we never truly lose those people; we may lose them physically, but they're always within us.

Ask Silva

Religion and queerness together can be very difficult to navigate, because for some people, there is an inner conflict between the two. While it was difficult, Mendez was able to make a decision that ultimately supported them in living authentically, but this isn't possible for everyone. What advice would you give to someone who is questioning, but is also dealing with inner conflict, to ensure they are able to take care of themselves and their psychological needs?

It is tragic that many LGBTQ+ people have to choose between their sexuality/gender identity and their religion. For some, it is impossible to reconcile the two, especially if there has been a lot of religious-based trauma (which is common with LGBTQ+ people). But for others, there may be a way to build a bridge between the two. My advice would be to connect with faith-based LGBTQ+ communities, talk to them and see what you can learn from them.

There are groups of LGBTQ+ Christians, Muslims and Jewish people. These people may be able to teach a different way to read religious texts and to help with reconciling with religion. There are also a growing number of LGBTQ+ people who embrace a different type of spirituality, often called 'queer spirituality', for LGBTQ+ people who are, or were, religious, do not want to give up on their faith, but want to take on a different form of religion that is more aligned with embracing their sexuality and gender identity.

CHAPTER 9

Loss of a Partner

Theo Parsonson

Age: 42
Pronouns: He/Him
Sexual orientation/identity: Queer
Occupation: HR professional and yoga instructor
Home town: Brighton, UK

Theo lives by the beach in Hove. He likes to practise and teach yoga and loves to cook. He strives to live in accordance with his deepest belief that the most difficult experiences and parts of life can be transformed into medicine through the application of the human heart. You can reach him on instagram: @futureforeveryoga.

In this interview, I speak with Theo about his experience of the loss of a partner. Theo is my husband, and as our separation was one of the factors that inspired this book, we decided to sit down and talk about this experience. Please be aware that this interview makes references to death, poor mental health, separation, sex and suicidal thoughts.

How do you tend to manage an ending or a loss when it's presented to you?

Not very well probably. I'm not sure I really feel now that managing a loss or an ending is really possible beyond a certain point. I think one of the things that has really struck me over these last few years is that a lot of the rhetoric that we have around loss and our responses to difficult situations in life is a bit of a comfort blanket against the elephant in the room: that actually sometimes things go wrong and there might not be a reason, and there might not be a way to sweeten it up and deal with it. Sometimes in the midst of a loss or any other kind of challenge, you're a bit of a flailing mess and that is unavoidable. It would be much nicer to be able to go through a loss and have a technique to take the edge off it and be able to stay calm and in control. That's probably what we all want. Most of us want a degree of control over something that we're not in control of, and that's what makes loss so frightening because it shows us that we're not in control. Sometimes, there's nothing to do other than to be a mess. Maybe sometimes you numb out; even that feeling is all about handling loss in the right way, isn't it? We can fall prey to this idea from Instagram and popular psychology that there is a right way to go through loss, but you do what you have to do in the moment.

We're talking about loss of a partner, and given the fact that

we separated last year, it felt as if there were no better two people to discuss this topic than us. What I'm really interested to know, first of all though, is how you feel talking about this subject a year on and having it as part of this book.

There's maybe a sense of liberation that's come about over the last few years, when your worst fear is realized. I suppose that's in the sense of our separation and also that inability to be able to control the circumstances of my life. It feels a bit as if there's a sense of freedom that comes after that. Why not talk about it? There's no image to maintain any more.

Do you remember the initial moment that you understood that the loss had happened, or that it was going to happen?

I don't know that there was one moment. For me, it felt like a growing sense of being out of accord with each other. I suppose it probably did boil up to one moment last year where it just felt as if we were on completely different pages, and it was not reconcilable. There was no way back to a place where the lines of communication were open. We were seeing the world in two completely different ways, and it was not really possible to reconcile those views.

What were your feelings at that time?

In all honesty, I don't know that I felt a real sense of loss at that point. I just felt exhausted, really. The thing is, it was a loss of the relationship, but it was also such a loss of all the ideas of what I thought was the right way to live a life, go about things, and all the rest of it. None of it had worked. I felt that we'd both put a lot of work into the marriage and the relationship over a long period of time; we'd always talked about the fact that a marriage or a relationship takes an awful lot of work, but before all of this happened, there was a lot of amazing stuff that came out of it. So, I didn't feel the work because I was feeling the good stuff. I just felt an overwhelming sense of tiredness really.

You talked about the ideas that were stripped away from the marriage. Can you talk to me a bit more about those?

The ideas in the marriage were really ideas that I had about life, and they're very deeply ingrained assumptions that we make about life without really even realizing that we're making them. It boils down to how much we're in control and I think I always had this sense before the last few years that if you did the right things, if you behaved in the right kind of way, if you had the right qualities, if you were patient, if you listened, if you whatever, things would work out and there would be a happy ever after. I could apply that to lots of situations in life, not just relationships, whether it's work, friendships or anything. It probably comes from the stories that we're raised on and also other societal pressures from religion and things like that. There is a collective set of cultural ideas that the right kind of person, or the right kind of behaviour, equals good results. I've been driven by those ideas without realizing it and also when I look around me, a lot of people are probably driven by this idea that doing the right things gets rewarded. Above and beyond everything, I've lost my sense that I can control the events of my life in any aspect in that kind of way.

Regardless of separation and the fact that we decided that was what was going to happen, from my perspective, there was sadness that we had got to that point and that we'd lost our

way. But also, I still feel that there was so much love between us both as well. Communication didn't suffer, we didn't treat each other badly, we didn't speak to each other in a poor way. Yes, we had to have some tough conversations and some real conversations where we had to acknowledge what maybe hadn't gone well, but I don't feel we treated each other badly. Would you agree with that?

I think you're right and that was one of the really sad things about the situation; it wasn't a lack of love or respect on our part for either of us that caused things to break down in the way that they did. It was just our own changing worldviews and priorities and dealing with our own individual stuff. It was an inability to get on the same page. You and I, from the beginning, before anything else was ever on the table, liked each other and respected each other. I don't think that ever went away, however difficult things were, or as you say, however tough conversations were that we needed to have. Neither of us ever wished the other badly or anything like that. I don't know if it's in our nature for either of us to do that.

I'm not judging other relationships, and maybe we're lucky in this regard, but when you have shared such a friendship and love, to go from that to hating each other and talking to each other badly just doesn't make sense. For me, it invalidates everything you've shared together. Even if things haven't gone well, yes, there may be frustrations and people have different things going on, but that respect you talk about is still so important because ultimately, if you've loved someone once or you love them but just in a different way, you want the best for them. You don't want to treat them badly. So, I'm glad that we

were able to do that. I think anything else would have been a disservice to everything that we'd shared and done together, if that makes sense.

Yes, it does make sense and to a degree, we built that together. But also, it was an individual choice that we both made, wasn't it? If one of us had gone on the attack to the other, then that potentially changes the behaviour of the other. It's a bit to do with temperament, I think; we are not super confrontational or aggressive people. We both tend to try to look for a peaceful solution. I think that's inherent in you as well; you're more impulsive than I am, but I don't think going on the attack sits well with you either.

So, we met when I was 21 and you were 23. I'm currently 39 and I'm holding on to that for a few months, and you're 42. When you get into a relationship and when you're that young age, it is a bit like a fairytale, isn't it? When you're young, you only think about the good things, about life together and building a relationship and all the positives. We're taught to look for a happy ever after, but inevitably people change as time goes on and this year it will be 19 years that we've known each other. This is amazing, but we're different people to those two who met in 2005. I'm interested to know, because as you know from my perspective, I would have done anything possible to avoid things changing or us never being aligned, but did you ever have any thoughts when we were younger or as we were going through our relationship, that there would come a point where there would be difference? I guess you can't foresee the future, but it is kind of inevitable that people will change over time.

I did have those thoughts at times, but also, this comes back to what I was talking about in the earlier part of the interview, around this idea of a loss of illusion. We didn't just have a super easy fairytale ride of it when we got together. We went through some really tough times quite soon after getting together. There were times the relationship was difficult, for both of us, and it's only human in those times to question whether it was working or going to continue, or whether something was going to go wrong. What always carried me through was that deep underlying belief that there was a plan, and we would be together, and that's what I don't believe any more. Not just between you and me, but in all situations.

It's a fundamental switch between spending your energy trying to control the situation around you through doing and saying the right things, and achieving a more mature relationship to all aspects of life which understands that things are going to happen, and all I can do is choose my response to those situations. I can't control them.

Things were difficult at times. I've talked about this in parts of the book, around the loss I experienced at a very young age. Losing my best friend after we'd only been together 18 months. I guess at that particular time I was having a bit of a mental health crisis and not really knowing how to deal with it. With a more mature view, I can see that what I probably needed at the time was medication and more intense therapy, but at the time you do the best you can with what you have.

I remember around 2015/2016, we got to a point where life became really joyful and easy. It was almost as if we'd got over this really bumpy time. We'd moved house. You were cooking loads. We had friends around for dinner. We were doing really

nice things, going on holidays, all that kind of stuff. And then COVID hit and it felt as if it all went to shit.

We've both said this, but there literally was nowhere to run, and COVID was like a massive mirror. We both had stuff we were dealing with personally, stuff that we needed to process and heal from, and we were both trying our best, but also both trying to keep the relationship going. In some way that was the beginning of things starting to crumble. Your dad had passed away during that time also, and shortly after, with no real plan or intention prior to this, we decided to move to another city, and everything happened so quickly.

We then got to Brighton and decided to try something different, to be non-monogamous! What could possibly go wrong?! Do you think the move, and non-monogamy, was a bit of a plaster on an already fragile situation, to make things a bit easier in our relationship and try and patch things up without really knowing what we were doing or how we were doing it? We'd been monogamous for 17 years, then we moved here and it was like the world was open, we were in a different city, and there was this vibrance, opportunities to go out and party and all that kind of stuff. Our world changed so dramatically, so quickly.

I think even that retelling of our story – and I've told it that way as well – is still the way of looking at the world that I'm trying to move away from: that there were times in the past that were bad and that we should have done differently or should have done better. You talk about the early parts of our relationship, where you were under a lot of strain, and it would have been better if you'd had different support, and then a time where everything was good. We did some stuff wrong, and then we did some stuff right, and then we did some stuff wrong again. But we can't escape the fundamental fact that you just lose sometimes, and that your best laid plans go wrong and you respond according to the situation at the time, with what you know and what's going on around you.

None of it is a failure. We apply that narrative around our lives to make ourselves feel in control because when we look back over the past, we think that if we knew then what we know now, we would have done things differently, and we'd have got it right. That gives us a bit of subconscious reassurance that if that comes up again in the future, we're in control. I think the same thing when I look at the last few years and the openness and non-monogamy. That decision came out of where our relationship was at the time, but also the circumstances that we'd grown up with and our individual thought processes. Do I think it was a sticking plaster? I don't know if I'd define it in those terms, because again, it gives me that sense of making a right or wrong decision, and I don't think that there was a right or wrong. It's just where we got to, and it's the choice we made. It had some upsides to it, and it had some big downsides to it. I think it just was what it was and is what it is.

So, after we decided to separate, I had a break for 12 weeks in Gran Canaria and you were living by yourself. Can you talk to me about what that time was like for you over the summer of 2023?
That whole summer was an experience of just being out of control at times. I can remember I would be on the beach or somewhere and I'd be feeling okay and then all of a sudden, I'd feel an intense wave of grief and sadness and I wouldn't be able

to hold a sob in. I'd literally sob on the beach, pretty much out of nowhere. I'd feel that I wanted to have a good cry, but then I couldn't do that either. It wouldn't come. So, the emotions and things had their own journey and their own experience. I wanted to weave a storyline around it and be able to do the right things to be able to process my grief in the right way and get my emotions out.

We were separated, so we were also at liberty to see other people. The emotions would bump up against my idea that I wanted to meet other guys, and when it actually came down to it, I'd find that I didn't want to or I couldn't go through with it, and I couldn't really understand what was going on. All my ideas about what was right in life, and in that situation, and what I knew about myself were really challenged. So much of it boiled down to facing that harsh truth that actually there's a limit to what I can do, and some situations just don't work out. I think that was the really, really hard thing.

When I was away, you and I had some really deep conversations where there was emotion, honesty and heartbreak; it was all there. What was good is that we faced the truth. I remember you kept saying to me that all we have is the truth in every situation, and even when it comes to us and what our future looks like, we only have the truth.

I know this is a really difficult point to get your head around, but it's still that subtle tendency that we have to look back on the situation and think, we got it right or we got it wrong. The flip side of that is when something goes wrong, people like to find a reason for why it went wrong based on what will happen in the future. So, it's like, well, that had to happen in order for me to then be successful in some other field, or some other way. Our need to look back on the situation and define it as right or wrong, and our need to look to the future to find the reason for the situation that's gone wrong in the present and wrap a narrative around our lives is just us trying to return to the illusion of control.

But it is really important to look back on situations and take responsibility for things that we would like to do differently again in the future. Through that new understanding of myself – that actually my need to look after others is both altruistic and selfish at the same time – I've become a lot more aware of the need for boundaries. I used to think boundaries were about protecting myself but I now know that they are also about respecting another's individuality. So, it's important to learn your lessons, but sometimes we have to give up the need to define a situation and just let it speak for itself. It was just a culmination of all kinds of factors, and the reality is, however much we learn from it or however wise our lives make us, there will be other situations that come up that challenge what we think we know about life and challenge the way that we normally do things, and they will cause us pain. The reality is that they're not wrong, they're just a facet of any life.

I really appreciate the feeling of freedom by not needing to control things. I'm still learning this, but I'm really trying to relinquish control. Last year there was just a groundlessness of everything, and there was nothing to hold on to, because so much ended for me personally.

Now I look forward, and of course, there's always going to be that need to try and control something and that human

instinct to acknowledge danger or that something's going to happen, but I think we have to really question our motives when we do that and understand why we're trying to control the narrative or why we're trying to keep everything together. I definitely think that's something that I want to change, not just in our relationship but in life generally, because it's a little bit exhausting.

Something that has occurred to me through this whole piece is that there is no difference between an open heart and a broken heart, and to walk through life in an open-hearted way is to keep company with pain.

In the face of what you're talking about, which is the circumstances of our lives and relationships with other people, they are going to wound us at times, but the alternative is to close down out of fear and not risk that pain and then shut people out.

What we need, in order to be able to walk through the world with the brokenness of an open heart, is courage. This need for control is a response to fear. We're afraid of loss, of uncertainty, and we're afraid of the truth that we all really know in our hearts, which is that we're not in control of anything and that life can change at any time.

When we feel that fear, we resort to these techniques that we think will control the circumstances around us, which is that storyline that we wrap around things that I've talked a lot about. So, these are all responses to the fearfulness of the uncertainty of life. The best thing that we can do is learn to cultivate the courage to face the truth, and to face the inevitable pain and heartaches that will come through life. I'd rather spend the rest of my life increasingly cultivating that courage to open my heart rather than retreating to the illusion of control.

You've put that perfectly, I don't think there's anything to add to that, to be honest!

So, we are now together again. We decided that we would move forward with our relationship, and our marriage, but it almost didn't happen. And then it did. And then it didn't. And then it did.

Sorry about that!

That's okay! I think that just goes to show that there isn't one way of doing this. You have to go with what feels right. I just remember thinking, if this is really over, why do we feel so fucking sad about it, and so upset? I know that it was a loss, and I know that it was a form of grief; maybe over time, if we hadn't got back together, we'd have processed that and moved forward, but it just felt heartbreaking. Despite everything, the one thing that I think was evident was that we liked each other, and we loved each other, and we're there for each other.

I know you've talked about not having the perfect way forward, but for me, the loss we experienced enabled everything to be torn down, completely to the ground. With this, we now make choices around how we live our lives, and already it feels as if we are living in a more independent, supportive, kind of way. We're choosing to be in a situation, rather than having to be in a situation, because we love each other, rather than not being able to live without each other, which is not something I think is true for anyone, it is just another construct.

My confusion at the end of the year was probably the final bash around the head with a hammer that drove home some of the points that I've been talking about. My confusion was really coming from trying to find the right answer, and one that was not just right for me but was right for everybody. I was trying to find that magical thing that would somehow set things right, so that everything would be in its right place, but it just didn't exist. You're right, what we discovered through all the intense grief and confusion at that time was that we still really loved each other, but I don't think either of us knew and probably still don't know quite how that plays out in day-to-day terms between now and the end of our lives.

If we get to the end of our lives together.
This is what I mean, at the end of our individual lives, you know, whether that means that we do them together or not. There's a sense of embracing the mystery of it; we don't know where we'll be in a week's time, let alone in a year's time. The way that we do our relationship now might not work in a few weeks, or a few years, and it might adjust again in different ways that mean we stay together, or we part ways. I think you're right; when you can remove that need to get it right or for it to look a certain way, then you're free to experience it day to day.

Do you feel freer with that approach?
No one gets to be completely free in life, and if you define that as your ideal or your outcome, you can't ever do anything or construct anything. So, in the summer of 2023, when we weren't together, in many ways, I felt the freest I'd ever felt. I think because I had a certain amount of income. I had very, very low pressure at work at that moment, and all my time was my own. I could make all the decisions I wanted to make; that was a really pleasurable upside of that particular time, and it was really lovely not having to consider anybody other than myself for a

while, especially after long periods of time of doing that. But a life of being completely untethered isn't satisfying to me. So, in some ways, I've had to return to structure and a more intense working life, paying attention to the needs of somebody else to a degree, and all the rest of it. There is less freedom than I had when I was on my own, but I think it's freer than we have been in the way that we approached our relationship previously, because we are both coming at our relationship from the perspective of individuals now rather than preserving the partnership at any cost.

From my perspective, I want you to be free to make all your own choices. Of course, there are things that we are going to need to agree on. We own our property together, so we need to agree on whether we move and commit to a bigger mortgage, whether we decide to take a holiday together and how much we're going to spend, things like that. But we can also have our own money, make our own decisions, go on holidays by ourselves if we want to. I want us to be able to have those freedoms because what I've learned is that when you're in a relationship, it doesn't mean that you are one person. A relationship is about two people coming together and choosing to share their existence in the most healthy, beautiful way they can. We won't always get it right and sometimes it will be destructive, like it has been, but neither of us should compromise or give up who we are.

Yeah, I think there's a tension between freedom and commitment, and I don't just mean commitment in a marriage, I mean committing to anything – anything you need to bring forward to manifestation takes a level of commitment. So absolute freedom and absolute commitment are mutually exclusive in some ways. You can't have them both.

The balance isn't the sticking point. It's not about finding the midpoint, which means different things at different times, but I think what you are pointing to is that there is a fundamental shift from where we've been, considering ourselves two halves of one thing, to seeing ourselves as whole individuals who are sharing elements of our experience and lives together. That's a fundamental shift in how we approach things, but I think in order to do that, it requires a dance with freedom and commitment and perseverance.

Do you think with all the understanding you have now that the loss and the way you handled it was unique to you as a queer person, and that someone who wasn't queer wouldn't necessarily have the same experience?

The older I get, the more I think that so much of what I experience in life is shaped by my reality as a queer individual and everything that it has meant. There are probably lots and lots of reasons why I have lived my life in the way that I have done, but I think being queer has had a far bigger influence on me than I've realized. When I talk a lot about this need to get things right, and to do the right things, and get the right outcome, and buy into that model, I think at least in part that comes from feeling on the outside of what was acceptable growing up. So probably there's a part of me that's trying to prove myself the right kind of person who deserves all the good things in life, because actually growing up as a queer person, that just didn't look as if it was going to be an option. It didn't seem as if I could have all those things. Whether those things are in fact desirable or not is a different matter, but I suppose growing up, what was held up to be a good life was not accessible for me. So that has probably driven me to do the right things, and behave in the right kind of ways, and be the right kind of person, and be socially acceptable in order to have that right kind of life.

So, much of this loss when I think about what it has meant for me has been the releasing from those ideas and ideals.

Do you think that we lived the way we lived in terms of jobs and career, marriage, buying the house, buying the bigger house, essentially living a very heteronormative life for such a long time before we moved to Brighton comes from the feeling that if we can just be like everyone else, or if we can just do what everyone else is doing, then maybe we'll fit in?
White picket fence, that kind of thing? Yeah, I don't think I had access to models of a different way, or even just a different kind of lifestyle. I mean, having a good job, a mortgage, owning a house, having a pension, and being married, that was the pinnacle of the right way to do a life. I don't think for a long time that something different even occurred to me. When I look back at it, why would it? What else did I see as a valid alternative? What else was out there? What other stories were there? This has been said a thousand times, hasn't it? But the stories that we heard about people like us growing up were that we would become drug addicts, keep ourselves secret and hidden away because if people knew we were gay, we could lose our jobs and things like that. The reality is, that changed quite early on in our adult lives, which was really lucky for us. But in those formative years growing up and looking ahead to an adult life, that appeared to be what the option was.

So then again, I suppose really when things changed in the early 2000s and civil partnerships and eventually gay marriage became an option, suddenly it was as if the doors were open, so we wanted to grab this thing and be part of this thing we'd been shut out from. It was our time, but the thing was, I never stopped to think if what was on the other side of that door was what I, or you, or we, wanted.

Do you feel with all of that knowledge now that your queer-ness, your difference, is a superpower? You get to choose how to live and remove those binaries of how life should be?
I find myself very reluctant to define things as good or bad. I think it has had distinct disadvantages. I also recognize what you're saying, and I do feel that it has given me an enlarged per-spective on life. Some of that comes from queerness and some of it comes from other things. I'm a very philosophical kind of person and always have been, so I always look very deeply at things, but I feel as if I'm growing into a greater sense of inner freedom from those sorts of societal restrictions and ideas and have a greater ability to choose how I see the world and how I choose to interact with things. A large part of that does come from the experiences I've had as a queer person.

Do you feel as a queer person understanding and exploring your identity and sexuality, and your experience of living au-thentically, have enabled you to deal with challenges in life, in particular around change and loss as and when they arise? If so, why do you think this is?
I don't know, because my experience of growing up as a queer person was wanting to have the acceptable life and feeling shut

out from it. I subscribed to this idea that I could get things right. So, I think in some ways finding the knowledge that that wasn't necessarily the case has come as a big shock to me. Everything that I've been through, including my queerness, has led me to this point of greater acceptance of the ups and downs and losses in life. It has been said before in lots of different spiritual traditions, but it's still a revolutionary idea: life is not about getting it right, it's about cultivating the courage to face what comes along. I feel grateful, for everything that's helped me get to that realization and decide that I want to do what is probably the second half of my life now differently from the first half.

What piece of advice would you give to someone who is experiencing loss right now or dealing with past events and trying to move forward with their lives?
There are a few things. There have been points in the last few years where I've been dealing with the impact of loss, where I've been mentally unwell to the point of danger, having suicidal thoughts and things like that, and if anybody is experiencing any kind of loss and it's bringing them to that point, then you must get immediate help. For me, that's taken the form of being on medication for periods of time and I'm on medication at the moment because of how unwell I was at the end of the year. I feel that's not going to be for as long a period of time this time because a lot is changing. But there's a lot of value in that and if your life is in danger, you must get help.

The other thing I would say is that there is an unspoken societal pressure to get over it, to be well, to find the meaning in it, to move forwards, to sweeten it up. Everybody around you wants you to do that because it's frightening to see somebody else going through loss. So, they are going to tell you that this had to happen because you're now going to do this amazing thing, or life's going to get better and your life is just beginning, and all that kind of stuff. This is because everybody needs to believe for themselves that when something goes wrong it's because a better thing is coming along. But that sucks the juice out of the experience of loss. It's also a lie – no one knows what's coming next. So, I would say, ignore all those unhelpful people who want you to do that. Sometimes, you have to accept that going through a loss means looking like a mess, feeling like a mess, not being able to do the things that you used to be able to do, and going with it to a degree. Sometimes trying to slap a brave face on it just makes it worse and actually you just have to go through it.

Do you believe in life after loss? And if you do, how long did it take you to feel this way?
Yes. I do. I've always believed in life after loss. But I think that we have to accept the mystery of life after loss and understand that it's going to look different from what we hoped, expected, or thought it might be.

Ask Silva

As Theo and I experienced, there seems to be a narrative that society has set over the years regarding relationships, coming from a place of heteronormativity, monogamy and what is seen as acceptable, but queer people appear to be

questioning this narrative and making their own rules. Why do you think this is?

Queer people make their own rules because we have not had a model of how to be in this world. In the absence of it, queer people have to make up their own paths, their own culture and their own ways of conducting relationships, their sex lives and their communities. There is much creativity and energy in this part of queer people's lives, which is wonderful. In some ways, being on the fringe of society has helped queer people in figuring out a 'life model' that works for them, truly embracing being on the fringe and making it their home.

Heterosexual people have a clear path prescribed by society; it works for some but not others, so more and more heterosexual people are open to what the queer communities can teach them about paving a life map that is outside heteronormativity and monogamy and adopting new rules that fit better for them. It is also worthy of note that some queer people do opt for a heteronormative or monogamous life; again, it works for some, but not for all.

PART 2
Reflections and Resources

My Reflections on the Interviews

I am in awe of all of the contributors to this book. I don't think I will ever be able to find the exact words that illustrate my true feelings, but it was such a thrill to interview each and every one of them. I left each interview feeling inspired, moved and incredibly privileged to be trusted to tell their stories as part of this book. The contributors have shared information and experiences that were not only difficult but life changing and sometimes affirming for them. I hope you as the reader have been inspired by these contributions, and they support you with where you might be right now, if that is what you need.

I had a few things I was interested to find out from the contributors, during the process of carrying out the interviews, and writing this book:

- Are queer people resilient because they have already had to endure so much by the very act of living as authentically queer?
- Has queerness helped them to navigate change and deal with difficult situations around loss, because they have already had to deal with challenges in life that being a queer person has presented to them?
- Do the contributors believe in life after loss?

While all the contributors had different views and such interesting perspectives on all of these points, through the process of the various questions I asked, I feel that the conclusion I reached as a result of having these discussions, was unequivocally Yes!

It was clear for me through the process of carrying out the interviews that each person had a deep level of strength and resilience, illustrated by their stories, and by the very act of moving through the world as they have done, and because of the losses they had to face. As Juno so wonderfully put it, they found a life on the other side of the wall.

Reflecting on these interviews, overall, I felt that queerness supported the contributors in getting through these challenging situations and enabled them to deal with their losses in ways that were unique to them. The stories illustrate how moving towards and through the challenges that life presents can not only make us stronger, but also lead us to opportunity, and living a life that may not have been possible without the experience of the loss itself. As well as being very on brand! It was incredible to learn that all of the contributors believed in life after loss. I found the reflection on this question moving and inspiring during the process of the interviews.

Something that stood out to me through all of the interviews is that queerness and living authentically opens a pathway for greatness, and a beautiful life with meaning. While sexuality and identity may have presented challenges at different times for the contributors, when they embraced who they were unapologetically, their lives became richer. This itself is something that anyone who is questioning should know – there will always be haters, people with opinions, people who make you question your authenticity and whether actually being authentic will lead to a good life being lived, but it is possible. Everyone will have their own journey and story to tell, but in my experience, living authentically is freeing, it makes you lighter and can make engaging with the world on a day-to-day basis a little easier.

These stories illustrated to me that loss can weave its way through life in ways that are unexpected and at times not considered typical. When something happens in our lives that creates change, I think many people will go into autopilot mode and deal with the issue that is presented; some will then reflect and consider how this change has impacted their life, and a loss may be identified through doing this, but many will just move on. Our approach will come down to what we are taught to do, not only by societal norms and the expectations set from where and how we have grown up, but by the closest people around us, with whom we share our lives from a young age, and maybe through our adulthood, our families.

Learned behaviour influences our approach to so many things in life, and loss is one of them. How we deal with loss and navigate our way through this is a very personal thing, and what we all need is support. A support that enables us all to process the grief in whatever way we see fit and on our own terms.

It is a type of support that comes with patience, understanding and empathy. Hopefully this also means we develop the skills and ability to provide this to other people too.

I think I have always been different, and this was evident to everyone around me, not only growing up but as I moved into adulthood with friends and family. This is not just regarding my sexuality and identity, but how I saw the world around me, and how I processed the experiences and situations that life presented to me. I always wanted to ask questions, find out why something was how it was and speak out if I felt something was wrong. I did challenge others, and I spoke to people poorly at times; I guess articulation becomes easier with time and experience, and this certainly hasn't always been one of my strengths. I'm still learning, but I am getting better at it.

I have, many times, attracted and mirrored unhealthy dynamics in relationships over the years, and ended up pulling away when I realised that this had happened yet again. I have left friends wondering why I no longer speak with them, and I have also been the type of friend that gives everything and then pulls away and hurts the other person. I am flawed, I have and will continue to make mistakes within my lifetime, but I am owning all of this, and slowly as a result, I feel like my life is getting richer, calmer, and happier, because the repetition of the mistakes is reducing.

I have learned to second guess myself a lot in my life, but I am also now learning to trust myself and my decisions too, and I know in my gut, the difficult decisions I have made over the last few years, have been the right ones for me. I have gone back and forth a number of times, questioning myself, but I feel in the place where I know I need to continue to have my own back and trust in myself, but it is still work in progress. I guess you could say I am finally learning how to live in the grey, rather than everything being so black and white.

One person that I must give thanks and appreciation for is my partner Theo. Since we met in 2005, he has always been my biggest cheerleader and had my back when I have needed it. Theo is also honest with me, and I really appreciate this. When I make a mistake or don't deal with something as maybe I should, he will tell me, but in a way that is supportive, loving and honest. With Theo, I have felt truly and unconditionally loved and I know he wants the best for me. Theo is a truly special person, he is kind, loyal and has a beautiful soul. I'm thankful I met him and that we have been able to find a path forward and continue to share a life together.

Something I am sure of, is that none of this is forever. We cannot live our lives in a certain way on the basis that something might go wrong, or someone might die, or that we may be too late because of a decision we made; we are all heading to the same destination, and as scary as that may sound, I think it is also really freeing; were not here forever so what do we want life to mean to us? I've asked myself the question a number of times, 'If my life is finite, and none of this is going to last, how do I want to spend my time?'; this is something I would encourage everyone to ask themselves when they feel ready to do so, it really does make you think about the choices we make for ourselves.

Ask Silva

Is there evidence to show that queer people are more resilient and equipped to deal with loss, because of the experiences and potential challenges they have had to face in their own lives?

There is no conclusive evidence of causation between adversities such as loss and resilience building. This is one of the most crucial unanswered questions in psychology and psychotherapy: the relationship between nature and nurture. Are some of us predisposed to be more resilient? Or do we build up resilience out of having to survive adversities? My guess is that it is both. Currently, there are scientific investigations looking at a specific gene responsible for resilience. However, as a psychotherapist, I often discuss with clients the coping strategies they have developed in order to survive adversities.

While all populations can experience loss early in life from parental neglect and trauma, queer people have the additional struggle to learn to survive in a heteronormative and cisgender world. Some of us find it harder to manage than others. Is it because of the resilience gene? Or is it to do with other nurturing factors? For example, some queer people face discrimination from their own parents, at school and later at work, while others might have had accepting parents but horrible bullying at school. Certainly, we know anecdotally that those who had at least one nurturing presence in their childhood usually fare better in adult life.

My Reflections on Loss

Wrapping up this book one year after the start of what was such a difficult time, I can look back at everything with a sense of gratitude for how far I have personally come. Did I think I'd be writing this book, absolutely not, but then again, I had no concept of what would unfold as the year went on, and how much there would be to contend with. I think that in itself is a beautiful thing; at times in life, I have found the not knowing really difficult, but I now see it as a relief. Am I completely able to relinquish control and trying to control the narrative so nothing goes wrong? No, but I am getting better at this.

What I understand, reflecting on my experiences of loss last year and also from listening to the stories of the contributors, is that loss not only provides change, but also opportunity. The biggest opportunity that was presented to me was to realize it was finally time to look after myself, have trust in my decisions and to have my own back, and in doing this, no matter what happened, I'd be okay, because I'd be there to support myself. It is difficult to trust in your own decision-making when you've learned to doubt or question most of your decisions from a young age, or warned of the worst-case scenario, that something could go wrong. Having OCD, which some call the doubting disease, doesn't help either, but last year, something clicked for me. Losing my dad, walking away from my family, and then realizing my relationship may not survive, I really didn't have anyone I could rely on except myself. Of course I had friends I could speak with, and my communication with my partner was still in a good place, because while there was pain, there was also love, and that is why the decision was made, but deciding how I lived my life and what happened next was down to me.

Taking myself off for 12 weeks to Gran Canaria was the best decision I could have made. I finally learned what it was like to be with myself, enjoy my own company and take care of myself. I essentially became my friend, something that was so alien to me for so long. I remember a few weeks into my break, going into the ocean and jumping in the waves. The waves were so big, and while I was there alone, I was surrounded by families and other couples having the same experience. As I jumped in the waves, I heard myself giggling and laughing; it was the first time I had done that for a while, and it was the most natural and authentic sound to come out of my mouth. The laugh was carefree, and there was a freedom in that moment where nothing else mattered. It was as if I let everything go, there was no loss to think about or grieve for, just that momentary peace and joy of doing something so simple, yet so magical.

There were times when I was lonely, times when I went for an afternoon nap just to pass the time, because I was counting down the days for my friends to visit, or I just needed to be that much closer to getting home and having some normality, but the loneliness was helpful, because there was nowhere to run, nowhere to escape my feelings of sadness and grief. I had to just be with them.

I have learned the importance of independence, of alone time and being at ease with my own company. Since my break, I have relished moments of quiet, enjoyed days to myself and have even booked myself a holiday. I intend to take a trip every year, alone, because I think it is so important to have that time to recharge and just do the things that you want to do, without compromise. I am aware not everyone has this opportunity, but I do think carving out some time to chill, even if it is just for an afternoon, is so important.

I have been thinking about emotion recently, and I'm aware that since last year, I have been very sensitive when it has come to my feelings. If someone says something nice to me or about someone else, if there's a cute video on Instagram, or most evenings when I am watching *Call the Midwife*, which has become a regular thing over the last few months, if a baby is born, or something wonderful happens on a Christmas special, I will find myself very emotional and will have a cry. I guess this is just because that is what my body is wanting and needing to do at that particular moment.

Maybe with the experiences of loss and change in the last 12 months, with writing and with talking about my feelings, I have opened a gate that I can no longer close, and to be honest, if there was a choice, I wouldn't want it any other way. I have realized throughout all of the difficulties that you can't experience true joy in life without opening yourself up to and accepting that at times there'll be sadness. I think we are taught to escape this feeling, to always focus on the positives and seek happiness, but I understand now, more than ever that we need it all. To lose in life is to have loved, to feel sadness is to have felt joy, and there is a richness and beauty in all of it.

I would like to finish this book by telling a story about a gift I was given by my dad when I was a child, a gift that has brought me so much joy over the years, and one that I know will continue to do so for the rest of my life.

As my dad didn't have a great deal to say when I did come out in 2004, I think deep down he always knew I was queer. Since he passed away, I have been reflecting on this quite a lot. When I was six years old, Dad introduced me to Tina Turner. I still remember him saying to me in the September of 1990 to come and watch this concert, because he thought I would enjoy it. And he was right – since then I have been hooked. I know most of the songs and dance routines, and cannot tell you how many times I watched the Foreign Affair Tour 1990 on VHS. My mum even had to ask a work colleague if we could have their copy as well, as the one I had was on its last legs!

I don't know whether this was my dad's opportunity to share something with me, or connect with me in some way, because in honesty, I wasn't the slightest bit interested in football, except I did love that the football boots made a fabulous high-heel clicking sound when you walked in them! I also had no desire to play with the tool bench that my brother would spend hours playing with at the weekend; it was frankly dull, and I just couldn't get excited about it.

With Dad introducing me to Tina, I think he knew I was different, and the fact is I was. I'm not sure if I really believe parents when they say they are shocked their child is queer, and that they had no idea. I don't want to generalize here and assume all these kids are camp or show obvious signs of being queer, but in my experience, this is a tendency. Dad, knowing I was different, thought of something that I would enjoy. He gave me something more than just a VHS tape of a concert; because of this gesture, I love music and dancing, and have always been creative. Watching Tina, then getting into other music and watching performances by other artists as the years went on, gave me permission to dream. Most of all, without realizing it, Dad provided me with security and a sense of belonging.

Looking back, I always felt different and, deep down, I was always aware of this difference, especially as I moved through my school years. I just don't think I could truly identify what this difference was. Tina and that concert was my sanctuary; it was a place I could lose myself in when I felt sad, alone and insecure, and needed somewhere to belong. At the end of the concert, she finishes the show by singing 'Better Be Good to Me', a hit from her 1984 album, *Private Dancer*. Tina walks up a giant staircase at the end of the song and waves goodbye to the audience. I only remembered last year when I was talking to someone about the power of music on my podcast, *Queer I Am: The Podcast*, that I used to rewind that part repeatedly, so she wouldn't leave the stage and the concert would continue. For me, her leaving the stage marked an ending in feeling safe and a place of belonging, something I was so desperate to keep, although I had no idea this was the case. When I watch that concert today – thank goodness for YouTube – the joy my six-year-old self felt is still there, and as pure as ever.

My dad didn't just give me a gift of watching and enjoying music, performance and creativity through this artform, he helped me to feel safe because of my difference, and whether that was his intention or not, I will be eternally grateful for this. Even now when I am having a bad day or feel sad, Tina is my go-to, and I think she always will be. I finally got to see the Queen live in 2009 at the O2 Arena in London and I took Dad as a retirement present. I am so glad we got to share that moment, and it will be in my heart forever. He did, however, tell me to sit down and stop dancing, but after initially following his instructions, I thought bugger this, and was on my feet teaching the lady next to me the routine for 'Proud Mary'!

Whether you are a parent, a caregiver to someone or just need something to help you on your journey, never underestimate the power of such a small gesture and what this will do to help. Queer people need safety. We have spent so much time on the edge, filtering ourselves, on high alert or hiding who we really are. When I watched Tina, all those things simply disappeared; I was captivated and, most importantly, I felt safe, and I still do.

It doesn't escape me that in the same year that I lost my dad, the Queen of Rock and Roll took her final bow and passed away in May 2023. Obviously, this is coincidental, but for me, the two people who gave me the gift of security are no longer around and left the planet within a few months of each other. I will be forever grateful to Dad and Tina for helping a young queer kid feel safe and understood, and I hope if there is a place where people go when they pass, they get to meet and party together – wouldn't that be fabulous?

Thank you, Dad, for this incredible gift, which 34 years on, I still find so captivating and magical! I will treasure it forever.

Ask Silva

What advice would you provide to anyone who is dealing with a loss in their life?

My best advice is not to rush to stop feeling pain and sadness, and not to believe the 'wellness industry' in 'curing' you from grief and loss. There is no cure because we have a human heart. What this means is that, even though the pain of the loss decreases over time, it might still be painful on certain occasions such as anniversaries, birthdays and holidays. There is nothing wrong with it. As humans, we are resilient, and we can learn to live with loss and pain, as long as we also make sure we have plenty of pleasure and joy too. We can still learn to love ourselves even when we're in pain.

Being queer is not only about surviving oppression, it is also about accessing queer joy and truly thriving. But we can't avoid the pain. When I think of grief, I often look to the moon. It was bashed so many times, we can see the permanent craters, yet it still shines at night, and it still influences our tides. And it is beautiful. The moon wouldn't be so beautiful if it was smooth all over. So, in our lives, we can live with our own craters, and we can still shine too.

Resources

Books

Roche. J. (2022). *A Working-Class Family Ages Badly*. London: Dialogue Books.

Van der Kolk, B. (2019). *The Body Keeps the Score: Mind, Brain and Body in the Transformation of Trauma*. New York, NY: Penguin Books.

Reports

Hubbard, L. (2021). *The Hate Crime Report 2021: Supporting LGBT+ Victims of Hate Crime*. London: Galop.

https://galop.org.uk/wp-content/uploads/2021/06/Galop-Hate-Crime-Report-2021-1.pdf

Stonewall. Facts and Figures. https://www.stonewall.org.uk/media/lgbt-facts-and-figures

General help and support

akt

www.akt.org.uk

Supports LGBTQ+ people aged 16–25 who are homeless or living in a hostile environment.

Being Gay is OK

https://bgiok.org.uk

Provides advice and information for LGBTQ+ people under 25.

Consortium

www.consortium.lgbt/member-directory

Directory of services and groups for people who are lesbian, gay, bisexual and transgender.

Direct Gov

www.gov.uk/guidance/advice-and-support-for-lgbt-people

Families and Friends of Lesbians and Gays (FFLAG)

www.fflag.org.uk

Offers support to parents, friends and family members of those who identify as LGBT+.

FRANK
0300 123 6600
www.talktofrank.com
Confidential advice and information about drugs, their effects and the law.

Galop
0207 704 2040 (LGBT+ hate crime helpline)
0800 999 5428 (LGBT+ domestic abuse helpline)
0800 130 3335 (Conversion therapy helpline)
help@galop.org.uk
https://galop.org.uk
Provides helplines and other support for LGBT+ adults and young people who have experienced hate crime, sexual violence or domestic abuse.

Gender Identity Research & Education Society (GIRES)
www.gires.org.uk
Works to improve the lives of trans and gender non-conforming people of all ages, including those who are non-binary and non-gender.

Gendered Intelligence
https://genderedintelligence.co.uk
Supports young trans people aged under 25, and provides information for their parents and carers.

LGBT Foundation
0345 3303030
https://lgbt.foundation

Provides advice, support and information for people identifying as LGBTQ+.

Mermaids

0808 801 0400

https://mermaidsuk.org.uk

Supports gender-diverse young people aged 19 and under, and their families and carers. Offers a helpline and webchat.

Samaritans

116 123 (freephone)

Freepost SAMARITANS LETTERS

www.samaritans.org

Open 24/7 for anyone who needs to talk. Samaritans also has a Welsh Language Line on 0808 164 0123 (7pm–11pm every day).

Stonewall

08000 50 20 20

www.stonewall.org.uk

Provides information and advice for LGBTQ+ people on a range of issues.

Stonewall Housing

020 7359 5767

https://stonewallhousing.org

Offers specialist housing advice for anyone identifying as LGBTQ+ in England.

Switchboard

0800 0119 100

hello@switchboard/lgbt
https://switchboard.lgbt
Provides listening services, information and support for lesbian, gay, bisexual and transgender people.

Bereavement support

Cruse
www.cruse.org.uk/get-support/helpline
Tel: 0808 808 1677
Provides emotional support to anyone affected by grief.

OCD resources

OCD UK
www.ocduk.org
Provides advice, information and support services for those affected by OCD.

Mind
www.mind.org.uk
Offers information and advice to people with mental health problems.

NHS
www.nhs.uk/mental-health/conditions/obsessive-compulsive-disorder-ocd/overview
Supplies information and support for mental health conditions.

Relationship support

Relate

www.relate.org.uk

Provides relationship counselling for individuals and couples, family counselling, counselling for children and young people and sex therapy.

Sexual health and well-being

Terrence Higgins Trust

0808 802 1221

www.tht.org.uk

Provides support for LGBTQ+ people worried about their sexual health.

Brook

www.brook.org.uk

Provides well-being and sexual health information and support for young people.

Mental health support services

British Association for Counselling and Psychotherapy (BACP)

www.bacp.co.uk

Professional body for talking therapy and counselling. Provides information and a list of accredited therapists.

Hub of Hope

https://hubofhope.co.uk

UK-wide mental health service database. Allows you to search for local, national, peer, community, charity, private and NHS mental health support. You can filter results to find specific kinds of support.

London Friend

https://londonfriend.org.uk

Offers services to support LGBTQ+ health and well-being, including support groups and counselling, online as well as in person around London. Provides information on topics including mental health, coming out, and drug and alcohol use.

Mind

www.mind.org.uk/information-support/tips-for-everyday-living/lgbtqia-mental-health/useful-contacts

Tel 0300 123 3393

Offers information and advice to people with mental health problems.

MindOut

https://mindout.org.uk

A mental health support service run by and for lesbian, gay, bisexual, trans, and queer (LGBTQ) people.

NHS

www.nhs.uk/service-search/mental-health/find-an-nhs-talking-therapies-service

Provides information about local NHS therapy services for

certain mental health problems. You can self-refer (England only) but you must be registered with a GP.

Pink Therapy

https://pinktherapy.com

Online directory of qualified therapists who identify as or are understanding of minority sexual and gender identities.

Acknowledgements

First, I would like to thank all the contributors. Euan, Jamie, Juno, Luciana, Mendez, Nathaniel, Theo, Vaneet and Zack. Thank you for giving up your time and agreeing to be interviewed. Your stories inspired me, and I know they will inspire and help other people too. I feel privileged that you trusted me with these, and it was a pleasure to have the opportunity to interview you all. Thank you for being a part of this project, and helping to create what I think is an incredible body of work.

Silva, thank you for your time and for agreeing to provide your professional opinion, thoughts and contributions to this book. It is a thrill to have you as part of this project, as it was interviewing you on *Queer I Am: The Podcast*, back in 2023; I hope we get to work together again in the future.

Jane, Harry, Will, Emma and the whole team at JKP, thank you for supporting this project. It has been a pleasure to collaborate with you.

To some of the special people in my life, for supporting me at a difficult time, and for just being there to chat and listen, it meant more than I can ever express to you: Andrea, Clare, Euan, Gemma, Kirsti, Leo J, Leo T, Morgan, Nicky, Sarah Darlin, SJ and Tarn.

Theo, for the love and life we share, the ups, the downs and all the adventures and memories we have shared together over the last 19 years; let's make some more.

Finally, for Jo and Dad, the two big losses in my life, that shaped so much of what was to come. You're not always on my mind, but you're always in my heart. I will love you both forever.

The Bridges Transition Model

When planning the structure of this book, taking into consideration the concept of loss, and the changes we face in our lives because of loss, I thought of different approaches to change and transitions that I have learned about throughout my career as a human resources professional. The Bridges Transition Model has always stuck with me and is something I have utilized when managing large change initiatives. What the model does is focus on the internal transitions that a person will experience when navigating change rather than the external change itself. When I structured the interviews for this book, this was a model I had in mind: https://wmbridges.com/about/what-is-transition.

About the Author

Andrew Flewitt, a podcaster and now published author, was brought up and lived in Suffolk, UK until they moved to Brighton, UK in November 2021, where they have resided since with their partner Theo.

Andrew is the creator and host of *Queer I Am, The Podcast*, a podcast that celebrates and amplifies voices within the queer community. The podcast has recorded four seasons at the time of writing, including a live season that was filmed in Brighton in May and June 2023. The podcast has been downloaded in around 60 countries and was nominated for an Independent Podcast Award in 2023.

Andrew has presented for radio, is an aspiring voiceover artist and is a proud member of the queer community. In 2019,

Andrew was a committee member for Suffolk Pride and supported the return of Pride at the Ipswich Marina after being absent in the town for a number of years.

Instagram: @fleweyactually and @queeriamthepodcast

All professional and therapeutic responses contained within the book have been provided by Silva Neves.
Silva Neves is an award-winning and accredited psychosexual and relationship psychotherapist, a trauma psychotherapist and an author, based in London, UK. He works extensively with queer people.

Silva is the author of two books: *Compulsive Sexual Behaviours, A Psycho-Sexual Treatment Guide for Clinicians* (Routledge) and *Sexology: The Basics* (Routledge), and he co-edited two textbooks with Dominic Davies: *Erotically Queer* (Routledge) and *Relationally Queer* (Routledge). He also contributes chapters in various publications and writes articles in psychotherapy magazines and journals. Silva speaks internationally.

Website: www.silvaneves.co.uk
Facebook: Silva Neves – Psychotherapy
X: @SilvaNeves3
Instagram: @silvanevespsychotherapy
Threads: @silvanevespsychotherapy